Art of Story and Humor
for Lawyers and Other Creative Types, Vol. 1

Catherine Berlin, Esq.

for Calvin

Special thanks to Katrin Jakobsen, Liz Cavalier,
Richard F. Griffin, Elizabeth Licata, Samuel Goldblatt
Elizabeth Slaughter-Ek, Lisa Nebbia Lindquist, Leena Bansal,
Marie Norking, Joakim Österberg, and Andrea Martins

Love to my mother, Mary Virginia Pangborn Lindquist, whose Saturday
morning adventures to the library started it all,
and Magnus, for the gift of time.

Contents

Art of Story and Humor

~~Introduction~~ **Warning**

If I told you that I became a lawyer because I liked to argue, chances are that whatever interest you might have had in my vocational choice would be fully satisfied, and you would start edging away from me and towards the buffet table. So let's try it a different way.

...

One night over dinner, when I was still in high school, I was relating some adolescent injustice to my family. After I had concluded my monologue, my father said, "You know, you're a glib son of a bitch. Maybe you should be a lawyer."

Let me tweak that a little.

One night over dinner, when I was still in high school, I was relating some adolescent injustice to my family. After I had concluded my monologue my ~~father~~ old man said, "You know, you're a glib son of a bitch. Maybe you should be a lawyer."

There is a back story. I could tell you about my Irish grandmother and provide a description of the dispute with the nun at school that had precipitated the dispute I described at dinner. Each additional element would add a note of interest, and, eventually, my anecdote would relay more information than "I like to argue" ever could. For now, however, I wish to focus on the effect of the edit. Does changing "father" to "old man" improve the story? On the one hand, "my father" has a distant, formal feel which plays well off the sarcastic punch line. "My old man" is dismissive and flip. I could try "my dad" or "my dear old dad." It is a more sentimental name, and that would also heighten the contradictions in the relationship between the authority figure and the person (me) telling the story. I do not like "my dad" as well though, precisely because it is a sentimental, intimate name. If I tell the story using "Dad," then it feels as if I am violating a personal conversation. It changes the point of the story by making the person giving the advice look bad, which is not at all the intention of the anecdote. Consider the difference between the best seller title *Sh*t My Dad Says* and what it was not called: *Sh*t My Old Man Says*. This is not a gripe about how someone I love has attitude issues and calls everyone names. No, my father recognized in me—as far back as my contentious, preening adolescent period—a quality that he had observed in others called to the bar. By saying "my old man," I am demonstrating what a flip, glib son of a bitch I actually was, and illustrating how good I was at provoking my dear old dad into uttering otherwise uncharacteristically caustic remarks.

For over twenty years Cate Berlin and I have been working together, and for mostly every day of it we've engaged in exactly that kind of word-smithing, chiefly practicing law, but also in our other professional writing. One time, perhaps, our writing was too good. A ways back, when blogging was still new, a lot of lawyers started law blogs. Some were specific to areas of the law— copyright blogs, blogs about appellate practice, that sort of thing—and they were good, but the juicy stuff was to be found in blogs about the culture of the profession. There was a site called *Under the Robes,* for example, that was full of gossip about judges. There were also quite a few law culture blogs about what it was like to be an associate at a large firm. When you think about it, this should not be too surprising. Associates are younger lawyers, younger people are more technologically adept, and large law firm culture is built on long hours billed by junior members. BigLaw culture has always been a petrie dish for complaining, in part as compensation for the princely salaries that BigLaw associates were paid, in part because everyone loves complaining, and in part because the life of a BigLaw associate can be a pretty miserable affair. Of course what they were really doing was shouting about their irritating, privileged problems, and although there is plenty of room in the vast rain barrel of the internet for exactly that, with loads more room left over for adorable pictures of cats, Cate and I thought it would be instructive to approach the shouting issue from the other side of the privileged mahogany desk.

During a brief fictional blog experiment, we created multiple old-timer partners posting exasperatedly-toned anecdotes, with the intent to offer up some common sense survival tips. We posted entries about what we wished the imaginary associates who worked for us understood about practicing law. "Read the file. Have you read the file yet? Read the file." "Don't ask *me* to think about something if *you* haven't thought about it already." "Tell me about problems when you find out about them, not when they get worse. Everything is more expensive when it is worse. Clients hate expensive." "It's okay to be wrong. While we're on the subject, it is also okay to keep some of you personal life personal." We had been there ourselves. We pulled from our own screw-ups, and we tried to illuminate through parody and gruff. The response was a firestorm. Traffic to the site started spiking. We were getting thousands of hits a day, but none of them were traceable to a referrer site. We were able to see the ISP addresses from all over the US and other common law countries, but no one seemed to be linking to us. They were talking about us instead, and it wasn't pretty. We were called "that nasty little blog" and our site was generating two sorts of reactions. The first was outrage: "What unpleasant bastards! What ingrates! Don't they realize how hard associates work?" Law students soon joined ranks. The second reaction was funnier, and scarier. People were convinced they knew the identity of our imaginary law practice, naming dozens of firms, mostly in New York, but some in the UK, and one in Australia. Friends of friends knew people who worked at this non-existent place. Some people had actually worked for one or another of the imaginary crabby partners. Then a third reaction surfaced: the voice of academia. "Why don't you listen to these old goats instead of vilifying them? They have been out there. They are talking about real firm life. They know what they are talking about and they are trying to send you a message."

Introduction

"Old goats?" Cate said. "Enough is enough. "I am not a goat."

Actually, we had had enough after three weeks. None of what happened was supposed to happen, especially the traffic and the "I know who it is" syndrome. We were the ones who had been educated. Our "story" experiment, no matter how well intentioned, taught us early on that writing well is like starting a fire with wet wood: It is hard to do, and once you acquire the skill you have to be careful. Fire is powerful.

So be careful. Think of what you are about to read as your first book of matches.

William C. Altreuter

Foreword
Beyond Sitting and Hoping

In the beginning of *Fundamentals of Good Writing*,[1] authors Cleanth Brooks and Pulitzer winner Robert Penn Warren drew a bright line. Writing based on expression is subjective, a method used for feelings. Writing based on communication is objective, suitable for instruction. Expression tells us why. Communication shows us how. Novelists rely on expression. Lawyers and scientists are communicators.

I disagreed.

This isn't right, I thought, pushing away from the computer screen, wincing at the calculation that I was a Nobel diploma shy of the honors needed to challenge Warren. Sensing failure, I became dismissive. I was not about to waste the day spiking my blood pressure over a how-to book. I have little time for a genre that promises me I can learn to save money or use less sarcasm in child rearing. Besides, the book was written in 1949, practically Paleolithic in a time of paperless paper. Why was I even reading this ancient artifact?

Then I remembered. It was the dog's fault. Four hours earlier I had taken my retriever for a walk, something her breed likes to do more than once a week. Because I prefer less exercise than she, I need podcasts to push me out on our morning treks. The day before, journalist Nora Ephron told me stories about working in the Kennedy White House. She was, she thinks, the only intern the very married President did not ask on a date.[2] For this trip, however, my phone selected something less *Sex in the Capitol*: a multi-panel discussion on the United States Civil War.[3] I did not think there was anything new to learn about that war. I was wrong.

Throughout the program, filmmaker Ken Burns and Yale professor David W. Blight competed in their worship over someone named Robert Penn Warren. That degree of gush and fawn over a man with three names forced me to skip the free-range portion of the dog park and head home. Public species like Oprah, Jesus, and John Cougar Mellancamp, people who need only one name—or insist on three—usually stick in my head. This time I was drawing a blank. When my search engine produced a result that combined Warren with "rhetoric," I forgot about war and clicked through to the online copy of the Brooks & Warren publication. "I hope they haven't stolen my concepts," I said to the dog, still at the door and still wearing her leash. She must have heard this as, "Ready for another 10 k, girl?" because the tip of her tail flipped up and down. "Soon," I lied.

Far afield from Appomattox and Gettysburg, I was now trudging through the rules of engagement for writers. I tried to ignore the Brooks & Warren instruction to put all expressive emoticon-types in Group A and all communicative tax lawyers in Group B, but it is hard to hopscotch over a central theme. I thought that their compartmentalizing was too rigid, and that such rigidity was the reason the art of story barely existed in commercial and institutional writing. I should have trusted the Pulitzer, though. A few paragraphs later, the men provided the necessary coda:

> *"It may be said, however, that, in the ultimate sense, we never have a case of pure expression or pure communication."[4]*

Exactly, I thought. Story concepts prosper when we communicators—we technical narrators—accept that our work also needs an element of expression to prevent boredom and avoid confusion. Not a once-upon-a-time type tale, but precise, compelling fact narration within specialized, professional writing.

Brooks and Warren spent five hundred more buttoned-downed pages adding that when we crossover well, our persuasive skills prosper, too. Exactly, *again*. It is career suicide to believe that persuasive talent should shine only during heated debates and beer commercials. Whether an author's goal is to obtain grant funding or stay employed, a writer's choice of tone, rhythm, order, pace, clarity, and imagery needs to captivate. Increasingly, software programs do our work, but drones do not have the capacity for persuasion. There are no algorithms yet for capturing someone's attention the way our human brains can. I checked. The scientists at Virginia Polytechnic Institute describe it like this:

> *"Storytelling is non-trivial because the space of possible descriptor expressions is not enumerable beforehand and hence the network of overlap relationships cannot be materialized statically. In a typical application, we have hundreds to thousands of objects and an order of magnitude greater descriptors, with an even larger number of possible set-theoretic constructions made of the descriptors. Effective storytelling solutions must multiplex the task of constructive induction of descriptor expressions with focused search toward the end point of the story."*[5]

I think this means we are still in the clear. Even after science gets the multiplex part down, our brains still differentiate. When it comes to movement, emotion, and surprise, science tells us that we humans still recognize and prefer the human element.[6] So here is the math:

> *Capacity for creating engaging communication + practice to the point of becoming skilled = an irreplaceable talent.*

Still, 500 pages is a lot of instruction on getting to the point. It must have been Brook's doing because eleven years later, Warren produced a single-sentenced, abridged version of *Fundamentals*. Asked why the Civil War continued to seduce the American population despite its ignoble basis and heavy death toll, Warren answered,

> *"Because the war made us great we like to look at it—as the dog likes to look at the icebox door."*[7]

I wanted to Photoshop Warren another Pulitzer. In one sentence, he shifted the debate on the war's causation and cost (unfavorable issues) to a new focus on the long term result of a post WWII America (favorable issue), and he explained this new focus with a compelling visual. The reader sees that dog waiting in front of a refrigerator. Then he pictures the kitchen and fridge, maybe his mom's. He imagines the refrigerator contents and what the dog might be waiting for. Maybe there is ham in there. "Hmmm, ham is *good*," he thinks. The reader is no longer focused on the debate. He believes that Warren knows about life. Once the reader believes this, Warren wins.

But Warren wins not just because he changed the focus of the debate and used a greeting card image to entrance his audience. Warren did his homework. He knew his readers. He knew they would be patriotic. So he moved the discussion into a favorable historical period and then chose the word "great" to describe the country and, by extension, his audience. By adding the dog, Warren owned them. Now he could dare to state his true conviction, a conviction with much less popular appeal: It is wrong to look for glory in that war. Monuments of treasonous Confederate generals and grown-ups eager to wear battle re-enactment costumes confounded him. Rather than state how he must have felt (something like, *"Well, the war didn't kill us all and united we are stronger, but we're sure not any smarter"*), Warren compared his compatriots to the loyal but intellectually limited family pet. We can get an audience to accept that perhaps, on one issue they have acted in error, been misled, or made a mistake, but we can never get this done by calling the audience stupid. Warren never called them stupid.

Warren's sentence bears an Atlas-load of persuasiveness, but is there a story in these 22 words? To accept that there is, we remind ourselves that the word "story" means more than the fiction section of a bookstore, not all sensory-loaded passages are argument, and less is more. Using an exponential method, Warren gave a narrative where the number of words the brain considers is many times more than the number of words used. Warren prompts his readers to fill in the fact gaps of the 100 "great" years after the Civil War. Readers' memories flash into Model T cars, the discovery of the Milky Way, or the sound recording of a terminally ill baseball player saying, "I consider myself the luckiest man on the face of this Earth."[8] They consider an odd lot of events, and then move on to the dog. It is the same with the hound. There is more to that segment than a floor, a door, and some drool. Each member of the audience will produce a memory of a pet that against the odds of success, sits and hopes, or sat and hoped. All this happens in 22 words.

Writers who produce fact narrations for a living can use this method, or any other method we explore here and in more detail in the companion session books, and stay within the boundaries of their required business styles. No one needs Nobel-sized technique to be successful, either. Because so few have trained in crossover writing, any incremental improvement can produce a competitive edge. In fact, incremental improvement is the most practical means of acquiring new writing skills. The week I discovered the thesaurus, I changed every word in a paper I was writing for school. I replaced my own vocabulary with the longest and least familiar substitutes I could find. "The teacher will think I am so smart," I thought. The teacher came to another conclusion. Walking is not the only skill best learned through small steps.

The steps are worth it, though. Even the best of us in our fields can stand to gain by learning story and humor concepts. One afternoon I overheard two discussions. In the first, a lawyer was describing his busy schedule:

> *"I am on three corporate boards, two foundation boards, and I am known to occasionally write an article, of course."*

He spent the next few sentences introducing his topic, how other lawyers work inefficiently and over-bill their clients. Two hours later, Anthony Bourdain of *Kitchen Confidential*[9] fame was charming an interviewer. Asked about the learning curve between making food and making a television show about food, he explained,

> *"I was always sort of a story teller. I liked telling stories. Suddenly people were paying me to tell them. ...It's like if you like to make model airplanes your whole life and then someone gives you an airplane factory. It wasn't a hard adjustment."*[10]

If I had to choose between the lawyer and the chef for a dinner partner, I would give a nod to the cook. If I were a junior associate or vice president of something and eager to make A Track rainmaking connections, I would *still* rather have Bourdain. To be fair, the questions did not invite equally compelling responses, but the lawyer could have chosen anything else to say—anything at all—and it would have been better than leading into an industry-wide criticism with, "Well, as people *know*, I *do* do everything." His message conditioned me to hear the rest of his talk as, "Now let's discuss what's wrong with you."

An audience needs to be impressed with us. We must be able to convince others that we have a clue. This is business. But had the lawyer been trained in story, he would have known how to *visually* credential himself. Make us see the glossy cover of a publication. "I'm on two Boards and I have just finished an article for the next issue of the *ABA Journal*." Better, offer up an image of a recent lecture location. Invite us to *see* the action, to be there. A hotel conference room setting is often the closest adventure the educational lecture series industry has to an airplane factory, but it is enough. Those of us who attend lectures—a large portion of that lawyer's target audience—will remember our own favorite conference and we will connect. Use a descriptive phrase that will help me visualize palm trees or a handsome tap room near a Four Seasons hotel. Use a memory link that will bring me in. Get me to where I think, "Chef? What chef? I could be more efficient, sure. I know where you are coming from. I'll work on the next file for free. Well, no, but I *will* be efficient."

We have every right to be proud of our accomplishments, but it is hard to showcase them if our brains are stuck in an "I'm just a communicator" rut. Unlike dogs that sit and hope, we all have the capacity to control at least part of our own life's story.

Catherine Berlin
Malmö 2012

Chapter 1
Humor is Easy

No, wait. That's wrong. Humor is hard. Seeing patterns in humor is easy, and that is our goal. Humor involves a departure from the expected, a 180° turn, a surprise. Humor is the Lazy Susan of literature, the spinning turntable that sends bottles of ketchup and bowls of rice flying. All engaging writers use patterning to get and keep an audience's interest, but to coax a smile out of audience, humorists must condense their passages. They must use fewer words and more intense shifts. The Greeks have a word for it, a paraprosdokian,[11] but these six syllables just kill the mood. Better to think of a joke as a linguistic reduction, a concentration of all the necessary ingredients that help us experience the pattern. Once we see these patterns in humor, the process feels more technical. Once we sense "technical," we become less intimidated. Less intimidated is where we need to start. Funny, and then persuasive, flow from there.

Patterning

"No animal should jump up on the dining room furniture unless absolutely certain that **he can hold his own in the conversation.***"[12]*

1. The End Shift and Anthropomorphism

Author Fran Lebowitz's shift comes, as a humorist's shift often does, at the end. It is a punch line. Lebowitz makes this shift using the technique of anthropomorphism: giving human characteristics to non-human things. We create patterns by combining the placement of our shift (the "where") with our shift technique (the "how"). I identify this pattern as "end/non-human acting human," but the name does not matter. I pick an identifier only as a guide, offered here to show that patterns exist. At some point you will begin looking for the two critical things: the how and the where of the shift, and then mentally file that pattern away in whatever classification system works for you. When it is your turn to narrate, you will remember you need the how and the where. You will consider the audience and facts, and assess whether any pattern you have discovered surfaces as an option, or if you should create your own. Look for Dave Barry's pattern:

"Lassie looked brilliant, in part because the farm family she lived with was made up of idiots. Remember? One of them

*was always getting pinned under the tractor, and Lassie was always rushing back to the farmhouse to alert the other ones. She'd whimper and tug at their sleeves, and they'd always waste precious minutes saying things—'Do you think something's wrong? Do you think she wants us to follow her? What is it, girl?', etc.—as if this had never happened before, instead of every week. What with all the time these people spent pinned under the tractor, I don't see how they managed to grow any crops whatsoever. They probably got by on federal crop supports, **which Lassie filed the applications for.**"[13]*

We again see the "end/non-human acting human" pattern. Again, forget the label. I selected the same pattern only to show that beyond the patent office and nanotechnology, nothing is really new. We can all do this, to some degree.

A very low degree, actually, but that is okay. We do not have to worry about becoming too funny for work. Even those of us who wish to be better at making people laugh already accept that despite a fairly dazzling chromosomal combination, a comedian gene is missing. We are long past considering stand-up as a dream job. We have avoided living on the edge of a police record and behavioral therapy. We recognize the genius insanity in comedic performers and keep some distance. We write business reports. Gag lines do not belong in anything we hand the boss. There are, however, different degrees of funny, and subtle humor persuades. In business we call it wit, and wit works. So if you notice you have the timing for humor, relax. It is a good thing.

If you are still unsure of the value of learning funny, or if you doubt that you can use such talents in your writing, consider for a moment the true beauty of what Lebowitz and Barry did. Lebowitz created a diplomatic, consensus-building way to say, "NO DOGS ALLOWED!" without using the word "no," without capital letters, and without an exclamation point. We need diplomacy and consensus-building in narrative persuasion.

Where Lebowitz led us into a circumstance of decorum and tablecloths, Barry went on the offensive. He attacked a hardworking, farming family. He approached the cross streets of Surly and Mean, a dangerous neighborhood for most writers, especially in business. Yet with the single-word sentence "Remember?" he invited us into his clique. Even if a reader had never seen the *Lassie*[14] program, she feels the pull to Barry's way of thinking. Some words have that power. Yet, it is not enough for Barry to say, "Remember?" and complain. Anyone can do that. Everybody does. No, Barry has to finish his speech with a shift so clever that we wish we had thought of it first. It is at that point that we are comfortable being on his team. We *want* to be on his team, regardless of how negative his message.

2. Litanies and Clever Series

A litany is a list, and creating a litany is often the closest a fact writer can get to argument without seeming like he crossed any line. Litanies are effective. They promote imagery by creating a familiar scene or suggesting an impossible one. The litany technique is a humor Clydesdale, a workhorse, and as it is with beasts of burden, there are many forms. For example, in the movie *Home Alone* the protagonist's older brother states three reasons why the thought of being left alone in their parentless house does not bother him:

"A. I'm not that lucky,
2. We have smoke detectors, and
D. We live in the most boring street in the United States[.]"[15]

We hear "A" and then expect to hear "B," but the writers chose "2." Then, instead of "C" or "3," we get "D." Perhaps the gag should have stopped at "2," but depth is not our focus. Here, we care only about the *method* of presenting the litany. This method suggests that the speaker is dimwitted. Another method will state that there are two reasons for something, but names seven instead. This tells us that we are dealing with an issue that is larger than it appears at first glance. If we say that there are a million excuses for being late, but then mention only one powerful example, like death, we send an altogether different message. This is not as bombastic and argumentative as saying, "There are no excuses for being late," but it makes the same point. To emphasize one item in a list, repeat it: *There were four reasons he had trouble getting dates:* **he was painfully shy**, *he lived miles away from town, he worked two jobs,* **and he was painfully shy.**

Humorists will often give us a series where every item is designed to shock and awe: *"He had everything he needed for college: an emo haircut and a selection of his mom's best prescription drugs."* These can be loud. A slightly quieter version only ends with the unexpected:

She liked the same foods as most girls her age: French fries, Pepsi, and **fingernails.**

My neighbor has three pets: a cockatoo, a Jack Russell terrier, and **a husband named Sam.**

A descriptive litany can be as serious or outrageous as the narrator needs it to be, and it is worth finessing. We know it is effective to list three items in a descriptive series—not two or four, but three. It is even more effective if we can work a shift into that series, as in the examples. We will later discuss how much we rely on logic for these shifts to work. For now, it is enough if we recognize this technique, and begin to think about how it can be modified to capture attention while avoiding clown shoe amplification.

Practice Tip: To use humor techniques in business writing, we monitor our pattern's volume. Volume is the degree of subtlety we employ, aided by the technique's proximity to the subject matter. For example, if writing an article on a new cancer drug, we work with the pharmaceutical industry's own inside humor, its unique visuals, its lab equipment, and lab personalities. We monitor volume by staying sophisticated and inside the industry. Consider the difference between the two statements:

1. *After six weeks on the anti-anxiety drug, the test group mice stayed nearer the perimeter of the maze and closer together than did the mice in the control group. The anti-anxiety drug appeared to make the test group mice display more, not less nervous behavior.*

2. *After six weeks on the anti-anxiety drug, the test group mice stayed nearer the perimeter of the maze and closer together than did the mice in the control group.* **Mice are not known for casual, detached behavior, true.** *But rather than acting less anxious, the test group did the opposite. They clung to the wall and became inseparable.*

I would choose the first version over the second if I am giving my employer a 15 second update. A new writing technique should never result in an unrequested sabbatical. But if I am a neutral reporting these test results to a group that contains at least one layperson, an insider conferencing with peers, or a competitor drug company thrilled with this unfavorable outcome, I would chose the second version. By using an opposite litany, the second version sticks without appearing argumentative or ridiculing. We want our audience to imagine mice doing what they never would: hanging out in the middle of a courtyard, discussing the day's ration of cheese and yawning over cats. Depending on the audience (and the opportunity or capacity to charm), we could even say out loud these items in the opposite litany. The distraction is just a blip, however. Attention must instantly return to the report. We have used the visual to awaken our audience, like a shot of espresso. This increases the presenter's chances of connecting with the audience, an audience who is now more open to the rest of the report. All this happens while maintaining a controlled volume.

3. Hyperbole and Minimization

Volume matters, yes, but whether something is subtle or loud should not be confused with the patterning techniques of hyperbole and minimization. Massive overstatement or absurd understatement has a vital place in humor. It can be well suited in business writing, as well, to demonstrate how inside that industry you are. To show how this technique works, we return to the dog as the comedic foil:

> *"Swimming was his favorite recreation. ...He had as much fun in the water as any person I have ever known. You*

didn't have to throw a stick into the water to get him to go in. Of course, he would bring back a stick if you did throw one in. **He would have brought back a piano if you had thrown one in.**"[16]

Author James Thurber placed the shift at the end, but instead of changing his Labrador's evolutionary history so it could talk or petition the government, Thurber's twist comes in the nature of hyperbole—a grand exaggeration—a common method that delivers anything but common impact.

Rather than state, "He really loved the water very, very much" (how most of us peak with our expressive detail), Thurber gave us a round-up. You did not have to do A to get B. B is an automatic. But if you did A, you would certainly get B. You'd get the entire alphabet if you did A. And here, for the alphabet—the grand exaggeration—where on a good day I might have exhausted myself trying to come up with "boulder" (dogs chase skipped stones) or "car" (dogs herd tires moving like free-range black sheep) as the super-weighted item to be retrieved, Thurber stays with wood, exaggerating it into a piano that we in turn envision in its rosewood beauty, bobbing down the river. The pattern is, more fully, a round-up leading to an end shift/hyperbole, and for all of its impact, it is anything but loud.

Practice Tip: Impact can be felt with minimization, too. Contrast your issue against something outrageously small. Take a business report, for example, where the figures indicate that an imaginary company is operating at peak efficiency, and its CEO wants to stave off grumblings for additional cost reductions. Ask the audience to remember the weakest of all business models:

Azon is in a position to consider further inventory reduction measures, true. Every company beyond a parent-subsidized lemonade stand is in a position to consider cost-saving measures. But as we learn from life beyond those Saturday afternoon ventures, expenses are a necessary item in a real business balance sheet, and Azon is a real business. Our figures show....

We could say,

There are limits to what we can cut. This company is not a curbside operation where Mom and Dad cover material costs and rent, and labor comes from empty promises made to a younger sister.

That example has more image and detail, but it starts angry and builds into an air horn blast. We could write,

"We have considered additional cost cuts, but the numbers demonstrate that our current expenses are necessary if we are to succeed with our current growth model."

Yet these are not words that condition an audience to nod heads in your favor. These are not words that condition an audience to stay awake.

In our Azon story, figures matter. To help keep the numbers in perspective, we used the quiet, familiar lemonade stand contrast to build a floor. Now, when key, unwelcome numbers are introduced, our listeners are expecting expenses. We are further ahead towards convincing shareholders to accept costs. They understand that we can never be on the ground, the zone of zero expenditures. We have created this atmosphere: Azon will have expenses; actually, Azon has to have expenses; and any member of the audience who disagrees with this reality is probably still living at home with his mom and dad.

4. Substitution, Senses, and Shift Variations

> *"Our house was always filled with dogs. ...They helped make* **our house a kennel***, it is true, but the constant patter of* **their filthy paws** *and the* **dreadful results** *of their* **brainless activities** *have* **warmed me** *throughout the years."*[17]

Helen Hayes, the author here, did not wait until the end of her passage to pull a shift. They exist throughout. Hayes does this with a substitution technique. In substitution, the writer selects familiar sayings with established connotations, and then changes them to suggest an opposite theme. Hayes started with the "house a home" and "constant patter of little feet" sayings, both associated with a warm and happy family life, and replaced them with negative dog behaviors. These smaller humor shifts add up. The substitution technique can be used at any point in the passage.

Where Lebowitz demonstrated her brilliance through diplomacy and Barry convinced us to embrace our mean side, Hayes' mastery surfaces in her use of another critical component of persuasive narration, sensory imagery. She triggered a reaction in four of our five senses. We hear the nails clicking on the floor, smell the kennel, itch at the thought of dirt and dog hair, and see the four-legged perpetual motion machines. She probably had an idea on how to engage our sense of taste, but, thankfully, held back.

If our shift is nothing more than a sensory-poking phrase, we have succeeded. We must be careful, though. A clichéd or overwrought description can flaw an otherwise solid presentation. It is worse than smiling with food in one's teeth (the gastronomical equivalent of chaos theory: It happens) and more like using the wrong fork at a restaurant or asking a woman you just met if she is pregnant (mistakes that signal we need more life experience.) A tortured or overused metaphor signals we need more writing experience.

Hayes engaged four senses, but patterning techniques can also impress by exciting just one, deeply. In the following six sentences, author David Sedaris, in a passage about his mother—a woman who loved to nap and who adored her dog—sends us to the Jonestown massacre before making us envision his mother as Marmaduke's mate.[18] Each evokes just one visual, but deeply.

> *"[My mother would look at our Great Dane asleep on the floor and say,] 'That looks like a great idea. Scoot over, why don't you.' A stranger peeking through the window might think that the two of them had entered* ***a suicide pact. She and the dog sprawled like corpses, their limbs arranged in an eternal embrace.*** *'God that felt good,' my mom would say, the* ***two of them waking for a brief scratch.*** *'Now let's go try that on the living room floor.'"*[19]

In fact, as we move into articles, we begin to see multiple patterns. Sedaris used middle/hyperbole for the suicide pact, and end/animorphism for the scratch scene. I hesitate to use Sedaris as an example for the same reason I do not use Robin Williams or John Oliver and Andy Zaltzman[20] material, or anything related to any *Family Guy* writer. These artists' free association-mania should come with the warning: Do not try this at work. It is enough to read multiples as proof that we can place our shift where we think it works best. In business writing, placing the shift one quarter to two thirds into the material may help maintain interest without nudging you uncomfortably close to a comedy routine. A punch line is always a shift. A shift is not always a punch line.

Practice Tip: Shifts and intensity matter. Compare these two options for a transportation hub coffee shop:

1. *With over 1500 stores in 20 countries beyond North America, Azon D'Lites has been serving loyal customers around the world for over 18 years. From South America to Asia and everywhere in between, you can count on Azon D'Lite for great coffees and sandwiches, and, of course, our D'licious signature bakery treats. So the next time you travel around the world, enjoy Azon D'Lite products served with a friendly smile. We will keep you on the move.*

2. *With almost 1600 stores in over 20 countries operating and expanding for almost 20 years, we know how important it is to stay on the move, too. Whether your travels take you to Rio or Singapore, a major center in Dubai or a quiet island port, you can count on Azon D'Lite for your favorite coffee aroma and signature bakery treats. Invigorate with a tangerine cooler or blueberry gelato. Got a minute more? Explore a mocha or cherry petite—a new dessert trend!—after a freshness sandwich on our famous protein bread. We'll*

get you there on time and focused. Your next move keeps us all winning.

Example 1, modified from an actual website, tells us that the company is dependable and global, with a popular product base and fast service. These are important business assets, but "from South America to Asia and everywhere in between" is weak. For text headlining a company's global mission page, we need more. We can start by naming specific locations that conjure up strong visual imagery, like "from Bogota to Shanghai" and we do this for three reasons. First, identifying a specific place makes it more likely a reader can see that postcard image. Asia is a big place. As we become more globally sophisticated, do not ask an audience to accept one image of "Asia." It is the same with South America. Send me to Peru in my mind's eye, or Chili. It is less distracting if you, the writer, deliver me to a specific location. If the location is obscure, then make it a café or beach in that obscure location. We can all relate to common spots, even if we do not know the city or island where they are located. We create an image-post to move us along with the story. Generalizations do not get that done.

Second, the use of generalized locations can arouse suspicion in the mind of the sophisticated reader, presumably the target audience here. I have been guilty of it myself. Once writing about rugs that did not originate in North America, I froze. They might be from India. They could be Turkish. What if they came from Vietnam or Pakistan? I knew only one thing. At best I could say they were Asian, and that was just wrong, especially when my audience was knowledgeable enough to identify the warp and weft of a kilim rug. We need to be specific to be credible.

Third, we want to avoid offending people. I am an American married to a Swede, and when my husband hears people say that something looks "European," he recoils. "We are not one group with one look," he says, and not always to himself. It is difficult to fully understand the impact that words can have on an identified group when we are not in that group. The risk in business can be too costly.

Beyond visual specifics, we double the message shift, and then add other sensory imagery. For example, take the original end shift of "keeping you on the move," and introduce it in at a natural point in the beginning, when the company was already talking about expansion (*"We know how important it is to stay on the move, too"*), then pump it up at the end *("We'll get you there on time and focused. Your next move keeps us all winning.")* This technique sends the message: We are committed to this value. Movement is in our system, *period.* Then fill the middle portion of the text with color, taste, and aroma, maintaining the readers' interest long enough for them to take in the sound bites about growth, service, and dependability.

The gift from Hayes, Sedaris, and the rest, is that we relax and begin to see more. An old humor axiom is "timing is everything." We read these humorists and react that way at first, too, thinking that it is all in the big shift at the end. Then we start to notice their other offerings, such as how and when they make us hear, taste, see, smell, or feel a noun. *Remember?* We feel how they hold us suspended from the second word on, and eventually instead of "timing is everything," we see that many things working together is everything.

5. Verbal Physics

In his review of "Mamma Mia!," *The New Yorker* critic Anthony Lane tells us how ridiculous a scene is without keyboarding the fighting word "ridiculous." He told us exactly what he saw, and placed it within the context of normal. Just as martial arts experts are trained to leverage to their advantage the force of that which is coming at them, this technique lets the writer show that a bad fact headed our way—true or not—cannot hurt us. We let the ridiculous work to our advantage.

> *"Sophie resides on a Greek island—**an island like any other**, where gnarled old ladies drop whatever they're doing in the olive grove and tunefully join in on nineteen-seventies Swedish pop songs."*[21]

By saying that this must be what always happens, we understand Lane's point that this *never* happens. We do this without launching a "no," "not," or "nej" into the air.

Humorist Mark Twain wrote an essay about how those of wealth were taking advantage of the insanity defense in murder trials. He was not a fan, but never expressly said so until the last sentence of his 1500 word piece. He gave us a solid clue about his feelings, however, before the end of the first paragraph:

> *"By the argument of counsel it was shown that at half-past ten in the morning on the day of the murder, Baldwin became insane, and remained so **for eleven hours and half exactly**."*[22]

Twain highlighted a fact that when read in isolation sounds too absurd to be believed. This was the first sentence of many where

Twain used sarcasm to support his belief that the insanity defense was overused. His examples became louder and more preposterous as the essay progressed. But his first shift—quoted above—is the most impressive because of its subtlety. It also served as the necessary stepping stone by which he led his readers on to his louder examples. He took the audience on this journey hoping to persuade us to agree with his own sense of frustration and injustice which he did not state until the end. Sarcasm is difficult to do without appearing mean, arrogant, or jealous. Actually, those words are used to define sarcasm. It is worth studying the form, however, because if crafted with restraint, it can be one of the best tools a business writer has for turning unfavorable information to one's advantage. The restraint is easier to master if we think of the process more as verbal physics than as criticism and satire.

Practice Tip: We can change a story's momentum by altering friction or spatial relations. We change the amount of friction by increasing or decreasing the amount of surrounding facts. We place the facts of the situation within a larger or smaller scope of events. This is especially helpful when we are not yet able to argue yet. When we expand or contract the circumstances, it helps our audience sense plausibility, or the lack of it.

Charles Ponzi's theory of economics is a good topic for demonstration. Ponzi began gathering investors by promoting trade on fluctuating international postage rates. He made the profits look bigger than they actually were, and investors started to spread the word of Ponzi's genius. Investors lined up. He would use the money from the new investors to occasionally pay out money to an older investor, to make everything seem solid. More often, he would keep the money himself. If we are presented with one Ponzi fact, such as "Charles Ponzi claimed he could earn for his clients a 50% return on investment," our first reaction to that statement might be to think, "How can I get in on it?" We are, after all, only human. Lots of people and institutions, all with lots of money, believed in his deal. With benefit of hindsight, Dickens,[23] and Madoff,[24] however, our next reaction might be more tempered: "On what planet is this happening?" If our job is to use only facts to get an audience primed for reality, however, we cannot talk or write like that. That is argument. The art of story helps us find a way within narrative guidelines to expand on this simple statement so that the public can to see the potential for fraud. We could expand the fact pattern like this:

> ***In 1920, banks were advertising 5% interest per annum.*** *Charles Ponzi promised a 50% profit within 45 days.*

It is a start, but it does not seem like enough. So we can go bigger:

> ***In 1920 banks were advertising 5% interest per annum. Trading in the higher risk stock market returned 10%. Ponzi told potential investors that he could do better than the banks and Wall Street.*** *Charles Ponzi promised a 50% profit within 45 days.* ***He promised 100% profit to anyone who let him hold it longer.***

We are still only reciting facts of what was happening and what Ponzi promised. We offer no comment on whether we believe it or not. But by setting the isolated fact within the larger scope of ongoing events at the time, and by including Ponzi's more exaggerated assurance of "100% profit," we can move the audience from pie in the sky dreaming to being more receptive to a claim of fraud. With enough facts, it will begin to sound too good to be true, even to the unwary.

This is a difficult method. It is hard, much harder than it looks. We have to build up and up and up, and then stop. It must be provocative yet composed. Few are trained to produce this way. Worse, it will feel overdone and at the same time inadequae. You might worry about jeopardizing your reputation for sophistication, but this method works. Another benefit to this method is that your audience will absorb and process the facts twice: the first time, during the narrative, and then the second as the matter is argued and certain key points from the fact pattern are repeated. The audience will see the entire event again, this time running through their minds in the background, like a movie. Detail is a seriously underestimated and underused form of mental media.

Detailing works well with even commonplace events, the events by which we are surrounded. If we are to challenge witness Lena's claim that she was asleep in her own bed at 6:00 on a given morning, we use her own story against her:

> *Lena said she was home and asleep at 6:00 that morning. She told us she awoke to the sound of the alarm at 6:20, and did her usual morning routine before catching the 6:45 train. Her usual morning routine includes showering, blow-drying her long hair, putting on a suit, stockings, and high heel shoes, doing her make up, drinking a cup of pressed coffee, toasting and eating her bagel, and walking six city blocks to her train.*

No one is arguing in this passage. Not until a later stage of our presentation will we state that we think Lena is lying, and that this timeline defies reality. Here our point is to to put facts into a larger context, such as a morning routine stated in freshly squeezed down to the orange seed detail, to prime our audience towards doubt. One problem with subtlety, however, is its subtlety. There is always a chance that our audience will miss the point. So, using our examples, we consider expanding further to make the point more obvious.

> *Lena said she was home and asleep at 6:00 that morning. She told us she awoke to the sound of the alarm at 6:20, and did her usual morning routine before catching the 6:45* **on-time** *train.* **Lena had to walk** *six city blocks in* **high heel shoes** *to catch her train.* **That distance takes a woman of Lena's height and build, moving at a fast-pace walk in flat soles, an average of 8 minutes from front door to train platform. Assuming Lena arrived at the station within the same minute that her train arrived, Lena then had 17 minutes to do everything else she described that morning – from pushing back the bed covers, through showering, blow-drying her middle of the back length hair, putting on her suit, applying make-up, making and drinking a cup of freshly pressed coffee, toasting and eating a bagel, gathering her coat and briefcase, and locking the apartment door. She had even less time to do these things if she got to the station ahead of the train. The process of making a cup of pressed coffee alone requires these steps...**

If you are lucky, several members of your audience waste four minutes of every morning just looking for house keys. Without stating that we do not believe Lena, we use only facts, including additional scientific studies and train schedule proof, to begin to persuade the audience that Lena's story cannot be true. It may not be enough standing alone to completely undermine Lena's credibility, but how do we eat an elephant? One spoonful at a time.

It is funnier when humorists use verbal physics to leverage their point, but the method is the same. It is a form of sarcasm, and widely available. Whether in an olive grove on a typical Greek island or an apartment in Queens, our daily routines are exactly that: routine. We can develop strong audience expectations out of common, tedious life experience. Boring but valid expectations give us a persuasive advantage in fact narration.

6. Criticism and Contrast

> *"My sex life is terrible. My wife put a mirror **over the dog's bed.**"* Rodney Dangerfield

Sometimes sympathy is our last best hope. We want to make the audience feel sorry for us, to nudge listeners into agreeing with us out of a subconscious, primal, protective sympathy response. One way to do this is to use self-effacing humor to show that we are loser jerks or that we come from a loser jerk place or circumstance, and we are doing the best we can to overcome our loser jerk shortcomings. This is difficult, however, because as much as society has the capacity for pity, society has a far greater capacity for despising loser jerks.

Self-effacing techniques help break down barriers and make others feel less threatened and more comfortable. If overdone, however, this inwardly directed belittling can destroy credibility. A self-effacing remark needs balance, something that is aided by contrasts.

> *"What if I'm not getting stupid? What if instead of elderly moments, I am having Einstein moments, like when the GPS directions say "left" but the eyes read "right" because some crowded memory cell is trying to remind me that the last time we took a left at that intersection, our car ended up as a float in a Puerto Rican Day parade?"*[25]

Go ahead, demonstrate the bad fact. Show the rough patch in life. Every person has issues. Every business has troubles. The audience will sympathize. To convince them to cheer, however, we must show that the person or business is otherwise worthy. When writer and producer Tina Fey tells us she was in the "gifted" program at school, she is sharing with us the fact that she is smart. When she is quick to add that no one would ever think to place her in a "common sense" program, she is reassuring us that she is less than perfect.[26] We like the fact that she is less than perfect, although mostly we remember that she is smart.

Columnist Gail Collins shows us how an "it is my fault" variation can be used to criticize another's behavior. When former New York Governor Eliot Spitzer resigned from his post because of a prostitution scandal, the columnist blamed the whole mess on the fact that she voted for him during the election.

> *"Maybe this democracy thing is overrated. What's the worst that could happen with a monarchy? I hear*

benevolent dictatorships are nice. At least if the dictator turns out to have an $80,000 prostitute habit, I won't feel complicit."[27]

Her self-blame is absurd. Readers would never fault Collins for another's sexual largess. But her real point hit its mark: We do everything we think we must in order to make good decisions, but we can still be undone by the bizarre, the unthinkable "Are you serious?" particles of circumstance. In business writing, however, critical self-evaluation seems as suicidal as blogging about your boss. When the stakes are real, no one wants to acknowledge imperfection or take blame. Yet holding oneself as perfect— claiming to be stainless—can have crippling consequences. To demonstrate, let's stick with Spitzer.

Eliot Spitzer seemed the tireless good guy. Named the "Sheriff of Wall Street,"[28] the only opponents worth his time were the corrupt 800-pound gorillas that no one else had the guts to challenge. He brought bad banks to their knees. If he had gone to work in spandex, many of his constituents would have called him a superhero.[29] Some probably did anyway. It also seemed that *he* thought of himself that way, too. Then he was accused of paying for sex. That charge alone likely cost him his stay at the governor's mansion. But there was more. As a public figure he had crusaded as aggressively against the commercial sex trade industries as he had against bad behavior on Wall Street. Soliciting a prostitute would have been just as hypocritical an action as insider trading.[30] On top of it all, he seemed to exhibit zero tolerance for human error[31] Double standards are never allowed if one is a superhero and super proud of it, even if one needs all that internal bravado to face down gorillas. When we take "human" out of the equation, including the very human traits of fallibility and humility, we risk losing the ability to connect with an audience.

Practice tip: Even the best personal, corporate, or institutional integrity can be bolstered in the long run by a nod to the fact that none of us can be perfect. No company's bottom line would be hurt by an acknowledgment such as, "There were years we felt as welcome as the 13th floor in an office building." In fact, it has the opposite effect. It is a door opener and a ratings booster. We all have had our share of ups and downs. Towards this end, controlled self-effacing humor, like a superhero personality, exists in a duality. The humility it represents keeps the near-perfect entity tolerable, and its audience tolerant of later specific and inevitable mistakes.

Exercise #1. Finding Funny

The exercises in the companion workgroup session materials are mental warm ups, conditioning the brain to stretch towards new narrative styles. I call this crossover writing, and it boosts the persuasive impact of our fact-based memos and statements. The session material expands upon the topics discussed throughout the book and helps put into practice the sometimes disparate-seeming concepts corralled here like wild mustangs, or at least untethered toddlers. Those exercises are finite and targeted. The exercises in this book are different. These encourage the larger, rolling, and more powerful tectonic "Aha!" moments in professional development, and it is development. No matter how large a group you are accustomed to working with or within, understanding and then mastering this art form is an individual and inward process. It is not a process you can bring to a group until you begin to own it yourself. Because "shift" is so critical to grabbing and holding onto an audience's attention, and because "shift" can feel like an anathema to a business culture of "No boat rocking, please," then "shift" is where we have to start. Humor is how we will begin to move continents.

Once we get a sense of the *how* and *where* that underlies patterning, it becomes easier to identify more methods. One way is to read the works of humorists. Humorists are dry and subtle compared to stand up routines and television comedy, and the patterns are easier to see and analyze when they are in print. Humorists' works are short, another plus, but finding them requires one to search through collections grouped by magazine, newspaper, topic, era, nationality, language, or, if he or she is prolific enough, author. Once found, we begin to deconstruct. It helps us loosen up. We begin to see why some passages grab attention, the process begins to look more logical, and the patterns and rhythms appeal to our technical nature. It is at this moment that we experience a paradigm shift, the moment when our norm is no longer our norm. We stop thinking that expressive writing is weak and sissified, to believing that we are the next Tuchman, Bernays, Tagore, or Agee. That belief, or misbelief, is all we need to get to the next writing level. We begin adding movement to our business writing; it changes forever and for the better.

> *"Rule 134: Every great poet has, at least once, described the ocean as undulating."* [32]

My own paradigm shift was tectonic, but more like the southern African plate: "I'm not budging for a million, billion years." On the first day of my first creative writing class, the teacher read a passage that used the phrase "rustling leaves." My brain began a slideshow of the big nature scenes that invite the same, tired adjectives. I closed my eyes and mentally dropped the course. This would never be my writing point of reference. I wanted words that quickened pulses when discussing real estate transfers and treaty compliance, and I would not return to a writing course until I read that description in a syllabus. I never saw one.

Years later, my long time friend and law partner, Bill Altreuter dropped on my desk a book of essays by humorist Calvin Trillin. I liked it, although I did not understand why. Trillin wrote about family life, food, and travel, none of which interested me, but within his anecdotes about barbecue sauce and children's theater I began to notice clever but quiet twists. This was new. No Monty Python absurdity, no Lucile Ball predictability, no misogyny, and no raging snark. He presented facts in a low-key, anecdotal way that made me smile. Trillin's musings sounded as my musings would sound if I knew how to muse. He never seemed to argue one point, but still, I began to see life through his eyes without realizing that I was beginning to see life through his eyes. I decided that we must have shared a common ancestor, because by the end of the book I had his attitude about everything. Most importantly, by the end of the book, I was seeing patterns and techniques I had never been able to see before. His was the perfect temperament for knocking down whatever barrier I had against introducing percussion and color into my narration. By the end of his book, I realized I could—and should—learn to write better.

Reading Trillin helped me overcome two obstacles. I accepted that I did not write as well as I thought I did and I relaxed enough to experiment. Relaxing is the easier of the two. Anyone reading this book is already skilled enough to depend on his or her drafting talents for a living. We have all been trained in the basics demanded by our professions, and in practice we have advanced from there. Shaking off the ego, however, is more difficult. A solid self-esteem is often a necessary component and unavoidable byproduct of success. We go through years of daily word grinding never thinking we need to improve. We need to improve.

Everyone needs a personal Trillin, or a Sedaris or Collins or Bryson. But finding him or her, or finding the time to find him or her, is a challenge. Welcome it. As Sarah Vowell says, we do get stuck in our too familiar.

> *"I missed the random learning curve [in school], how one day you're counting haiku syllables and the next day they have you constructing solar-powered hot dog roasters out of tinfoil. Being a grown up requires a twelve-month calendar, and that calendar is mostly filled up with doing things you know how to do."*[33]

Finding a humorist who shares your voice and temperament is a fairly pleasant homework assignment. We can feel less guilty reading on the beach or hammock. We *have* to. We tell our families the mortgage payment depends upon it. Soon enough we move into audible books and podcasts. Our commute to work or cross-country drive to the brother-in-law's house seems less unfortunate when we can disappear into another's sarcasm.

I take the night shift on vacation drives, those shifts where I dig in the bottom of my travel bag for random stay awake caffeine supplements, I cross so many borders I no longer recognize road signs, and I wonder what to tell the family when I run out of gas in a place that under a full moon looks like scary Transylvania or scarier still Alabama. I take that driving shift because it is the only way some stranger can read to me for eight uninterrupted hours. On one trip, I listened to the disc version of *Fierce Pajamas: An Anthology of Humor Writing from The New Yorker.*[34] The material was so concentrated and I held so captive by both text and seat belt that by dawn, an improv company had moved into my head. In this one overnight lesson, I gained the capacity to change voices. I could write like a skinflint dry cleaner or a confused sixty year old male homeowner. A week later I wrote a piece about airline travel from the perspective of a young, insufferable female passenger, admittedly less of a stretch. My husband said it was the funniest thing he had ever read, ever, by anyone. I suspect he has a bias. I also suspect that the damage done to my body on these many interstate all-nighters has aged me faster than a pack a day cigarette habit, but it is a small price to pay for the only compliment I am actually willing to die for.

As you are exploring your own sources of humor material, you will quickly find a comfort zone. Two more words of advice. First, keep it smart. Sexist, racist, look over your shoulder to see who is listening-type humor can be less funny than shocking, and alienates rather than persuades. We are trying to accustom our brains to business-based narrative. Second, if you dislike what you are reading, look for something else. The reason for these admonitions is the same. Any good sports coach nowadays will bark at parents,

"Never tell a kid what she is doing wrong. It only makes her brain repeat that wrong. We don't want the brain repeating wrong. Only emphasize what the kid is doing right. Right, right, right. Got it?"

The same applies here. Our time is too short and the learning curve too long to be subconsciously internalizing potty humor or reading patterns that do not speak to us. Of course, these are all just principles, not rules. If smut is the only material that does not bore or annoy you, then go with it. Just make sure you pay extra attention to the section in Chapter 5 on peer review and editing, and try not to speak too often at big conventions.

Once we have a few patterns in our heads, we are almost ready to begin developing our own individual style of humor. In fact, we can go ahead and try to mimic some of our favorite writers, creating litanies and experimenting with other humor patterns we discover, such as the Full Circle and the Weave. But success with our individual styles requires us to be comfortable with the writing concept we will explore in the next chapter: logic. Fortunately, logic is easy. No, wait...

Chapter 2
What Mr. Spock and Donald Duck Have in Common

Everybody's Doing It

"That is the way humor is set up, the joke is the play on words, it is the unexpected, it's upticking in a direction and—suddenly out of the blue comes the stunning moment where it completely contradicts the whole reality of the set up before, and then it is funny. That's what composers do. That's what performers do. That's what storytellers do." Yo Yo Ma.[35]

Comedians do not own exclusive rights to patterning. A pattern is the means by which all noteworthy expression shifts and captivates. We focused on humor initially and canines primarily because the shift is clear in comedy, and clearer still with some consistency in the subject matter. Yet beyond the joke and the family dog, all inspiring compositions require internal shifts. Yo Yo Ma uses patterning when composing each musical frame. Robert McKee, author of the bible on screenwriting, *Story*, insists on a shift, which he describes as a change in direction that should happen between the beginning and end of every movie scene.

> *"For a typical film, a writer will choose 40 to 60 story events, or as they are commonly known, 'scenes.' Ideally, every scene is a true story event. Look closely at each scene you have written and ask, 'What value is at stake in my character's life at this moment, love, truth, what? How is that value charged at the top of the scene, positive, negative, some of both?' Take a note. Next turn to the close of the scene and ask, 'Where now is this value, positive, negative, both?' Take a note and compare. If the answer you write down at the end of the scene is the same note you took at the opening, you now have another question to as, 'Why is this scene in my script?'"[36]*

Consider the value charges that alternate between positive and negative in this story about Sun Tsu, the author of *The Art of War*,[37] a 2500 year old book still on the reading list at The United States Military Academy at West Point. After Tsu wrote his book, news of his insight began to spread, grabbing the attention of the king of Tsu's Chinese state. Seeking to test the author, and perhaps be entertained in the process, the King asked Tsu to demonstrate his methods of instructing soldiers. Tsu agreed. The king next asked if

Tsu would demonstrate his techniques using women as soldiers. Tsu again agreed, and the king sent 180 females from the palace to the courtyard. Tsu divided them into two groups, placing one of the King's favorite concubines as an officer for each group.

Tsu then instructed the women, "When I say 'left turn,' you must turn left. When I say 'right turn' you must turn right." The women said they understood and agreed to follow the instruction. Tsu commanded, "Right turn!" but the women only laughed. Tsu looked at them and said, "If words of command are not clear and distinct, if orders are not thoroughly understood, then the general is to blame." He repeated the instructions, and the women said that they understood. Tsu commanded, "Left turn!" Again the women laughed.

Tsu waited until the noise quieted. "If words of command are not clear and distinct, if orders are not thoroughly understood, then the general is to blame. But if his orders are *clear* and the soldiers nevertheless disobey, then it is the fault of their officers," he said, then immediately ordered the two lead concubines to be beheaded. The king, who had been watching, became disturbed at the thought of his loss and asked Tsu to spare the two favorites. Tsu said, "Having once received His Majesty's commission to be general of his forces in that capacity, I am unable to accept." The first two concubines were executed and Tsu replaced them. Now, as Tsu issued instructions, the women moved exactly as told.

At the conclusion of the drills, Tsu reported to the king that the solders were ready for inspection. "Bid them go through fire and water and they will not now disobey." The King, who was now miserable, declined to come down and review. Tsu replied, "The king is only fond of words and cannot translate them into deeds."

Hearing this, the king paused. He thought about what Tsu had taught everyone and made him a general.[38]

Patterning tools are not just for laughs. There was a reason James Clavell included this story in his forward of the 1983 edition of Tsu's masterpiece. I experienced this reason. The shifts in this introductory passage were practically explosions, and I moved from thinking I was about to read a West Point novelty item to understanding why this book has survived almost three millennia. The slim manuscript was pure power. To this day, when I hear my GPS say, "Turn right at next intersection," I am one boot camp day removed from replying, "Sir! Yes, Sir!"

The beauty of such power, however, is also a curse. We read these stories and think that ours will never compare. We never even try. Tsu's is the stuff that stories are made out of, not our last business trip to Topeka. Yet even without concubines and kings, we have stories. If we learn to tell them, those within our respective industries will notice. Our small movements will be appreciated. A well told story, on any subject, gathers respect.

McKee directs his students to change the value-charge in every scene. Ma encourages a shift in musical composition. Business writing is no exception. We must grow comfortable creating interest in what we say. We need this interest. We want the reader to care about how our facts unfold. Whether dealing with transportation hubs or the number of Number 2 pencils we should have in our inventory, we do not want to bore. So we gather and review the facts, assessing which values relate to the issues at hand. We then consider how to structure the statement of facts. We use favorable facts as the frame of our story, and turn to bad, potentially contrary, or unusual facts to create the dynamic. The bad is often the perfect catalyst for the shift. The bad also builds credibility. Decision-makers understand that there are multiple facets in every story and rarely does everything swing in the proponent's favor. So, it is worth repeating: good things come from facing up to your weakest point.

The Law of Plausible Impossibility

Fortunately for us, effective, credible patterning requires logic. If we present our facts in a logical, rational, sensible way, then the reader is more likely to accept them as true. But it is a mistake to equate logical thinking with dull business writing. Without an element of movement or breadth, we have only analog communication that is *poke my eyeballs out before I have to read any more of this report*-boring and, worse, timid. To help loosen up your pen, consider this: Walt Disney understood people. Walt Disney understood business.

When explaining certain principles of cartoon animation, Walt Disney introduced his television audience to "the plausible impossible."[39] The phrase may be unfamiliar, but you probably grasped the concept about the time your mother switched you over to solid food. Disney artists would draw a character doing something against the laws of nature (impossible), but stage it in a way that made the action seem rational (plausible). If we pull a cartoon cow's tail, for example, we accept the fact that a bell around the animal's neck could clang. Why? It would not really happen, but the tail and the neck are connected by a spine. An impulse section of our brain perceives this as plausible because a more scholarly section of our head understands that at least there is the anatomical connection. We allow Mickey Mouse's body to squash into a pancake as he rides up an elevator because we experience a squish, too, every time we hit the "up" button. We recognize the sensation. If we believe that Donald Duck is frightened enough after running off a cliff, we will allow him to turn his body around in mid-air and run back to safety (fear and adrenaline), or if climbing fast enough, continue to climb upward into the sky long after he has stepped past the last rung of a ladder (momentum). The plausible impossible also gives life to inanimate objects. A car can come alive once the cartoonists have replaced the front grill with a mouth, the headlights with nostrils, and the windshield with sunglasses. We accept the outlandish as long as the artists have anchored the fantasy into a universally recognized fact or understanding. In short, there is enough logic to support what cannot be.

What qualifies as "enough logic" depends on genre, message, and audience, and we learn the answer with practice. But once we see that logic matters, even in a story form as light-hearted as cartoons, we begin to see how our strength in logical thinking becomes our strength in creative writing. We begin to feel more comfortable with the concept of story narration in business writing. The litany example in Chapter 1, "My neighbor has three pets: a cockatoo, a Jack Russell terrier, and a husband named Sam," only works because of a universal understanding that spouses can be reduced to other roles. To say, "My neighbor has three pets: a cockatoo, a Jack Russell terrier, and an airplane," does not work. Absent additional context, we cannot logically accept the airplane as a pet, so it fails. If I am writing a vampire novel and working within established vampiric physical traits, I cannot ask my audience to suddenly accept a scene where my night creature is sunbathing at the beach. Within the framework of my story, it is illogical. It does not compute.

Logic is not just for argument and debate. Facts need to fit together logically. In argument, we use logic to prove a conclusion:

> *A.*
> *1. All mammals are warm blooded.*
> *2. A dog is a mammal.*
> *3. All dogs are warm blooded.*

If the premise A1 is true and the premise A2 is true, then we use logic to draw the ultimate conclusion of A3. Because we readily accept the scientific premises in Example A, the conclusion, A3, sticks, fast. We accept it without hesitation. Here is another:

> *B.*
> *1. My dog barks at all strangers.*
> *2. My dog did not bark when someone came into the house and took our computer.*
> *3. Our computer was stolen by someone we knew.*

Here, B1 and B2 can lead to B3, but the conclusion feels less secure than A3. What if either the dog or the owner slept through the burglary or the perpetrator knew how to silence a dog? This is where narrative logic matters. Look at more facts to support or attack each premise. For example, if you want to strengthen B2, consider adding more information:

> *"Our alarm works only with the house doors. The burglar came in through an open window in my older brother's*

room. My brother is at college now, but our dog still sleeps by his bed. Whoever stole the computers would have had to walk by the dog twice to get in and out of the house."

This additional information makes the B3 conclusion feel more likely. Logical consistency also matters if you are looking at information that does not support the conclusion. Consider this contrary fact, a statement from the crime victim's friend:

"You ran your dog for an hour after you got home from school, and when I stopped over to see you, you laughed because Coco was too tired to eat. That dog never misses a meal."

If you are trying to prove B3, this is a bad fact. It interferes with your intended flow of the syllogism. It does not support the conclusion. It says that the dog may not have been alert that evening when the burglary occurred. Yet it is logically consistent with the issues in the story. A fact that suggests that the dog was too tired to hear a stranger enter the house matters to our story line. Now if we still want to encourage the audience to accept premise B2, we will have to introduce additional logically relevant facts:

"Yeah, but she was back to her usual self later. She was barking at every strange sound from the street."

Whether this is enough to save the B conclusion we do not know. This teaches us something else about the art of the story: we need logic *and* we must deliver it well. A story must be concise and coherent. Too many facts, regardless of connection, can make a report sound contrived—too convenient to be true. Our brains do not always want to work harder than seeing a cow's tail pulled and hearing the bell clang. If forced to work too hard by having to think about an ever expanding collection of facts, our brains will respond by rejecting everything. On the other hand, we cannot rush to any conclusion. A story must have enough information to support the premises, and be supported so strongly that our conclusion feels more like an Example A ("all dogs are warm-blooded") than Example B ("the burglar is someone we know").

Too few facts creates a different problem. Rushing to conclusions is bad, and we know what that sounds like:

> *C*
> 1. *Eric believes in a luxury tax.*
> 2. *Eric is a socialist.*

Logic cannot get us from C1 to C2. This is a generalization, an enthymeme, a conclusion based on one inadequate premise. Avoid them at all costs. These are where we find misleading bias, crippling frustrations and dangerous optimism, and they can work in the short term but ultimately destroy credibility. To support or attack the leap from the C1 premise to the C2 conclusion, return to the concept of logical fact narration. Use more facts to create the missing premises. Build out steps C1(a) to C1(j) that bridge us logically to C2. The same "build out" method can be used to suggest that we can never get to the conclusion someone else has urged. Critical facts are either missing or just as likely to lead us to other conclusions.

More pragmatically, never use the words "enthymeme," "premise," and "consistency" while building out your facts. Forget them. When it comes to logic, just think "my dog is a mammal," and you will remember what to do.

The One-Word Theme

Logic is the core of all captivating and credible writing, from fiction and non-fiction to whatever it is that Alan Greenspan utters. This is good news. If we are logical, we can introduce an element of movement into our writing. To do this, we communicators must learn that there are many ways to narrate logically, and producing brittle dry material or purely regurgitated content are only two bad ways. The first step in creating an engaging logical narrative, however, can be the most difficult. We must reduce our project to a one-word theme:

Overrun
Pink
Benign
Dairy
Outlier

Simple or complex, divisive or unifying, the theme is the constant, the line that supports the narrative account and survives throughout, from what color is the "new black," to why the sample group returned unanticipated results. Once we have our theme, we draw the box that contains the relevant and material information. For people who, like me, see all the trees in all the forests, settling on one theme that unites can be a struggle, but it is necessary. Without a theme, your report is nothing more than a collection of random facts that dies on the boss's desk. Rather than providing information, the un-themed report results in one question: "What's your point?"

What Mr. Spock and Donald Duck Have in Common

I first heard about theme at a course offered by the National Institute of Trial Advocacy. A tall lawyer with an American Southern drawl boomed across the classroom, *"THE FIRST THANG YOU HAVE TO DO IS COME UP WITH A THEME."* Then he wrote "Theme" on the chalk board. I stared at the word with the same empty gaze I have for Calculus problems. I suspected he knew what he was talking about. I also guessed, with astounding accuracy, that this would be a difficult process for me. He was asking us to crossover into the right hemisphere arena of short stories and novels. Once again, my brain reacted with resistance, and finding a theme remains a challenge. Recently I was working on a legal project, unable to coordinate all the facts I had been gathering. I stepped away from it, doing what I do best. I distracted myself. I picked up an article by Francis Ford Coppola:

> *"When you make a movie, always try to discover what the theme of the movie is in one or two words. Every time I made a film, I always knew what I thought the theme was, the core, in one word. In <u>The Godfather</u>, it was succession. In <u>The Conversation</u>, it was privacy. In <u>Apocalypse</u>, it was morality."*[40]

Before I could start fussing over how I had completely missed the essence of his creative intent, it hit me. I had spent weeks engaged in complicated fact investigation, but had forgotten to create my theme. Within two hours, I had my one word descriptor and the strategy I needed to move forward.

Do not create the theme until you have a comprehensive understanding of the facts. Otherwise something later discovered may not fit well. It will look like a handful of jigsaw puzzle pieces forced into the wrong places. Their presence will destroy the image you want to create. Another risk with theme creation is bias. It is a big risk, actually. We have to be careful how we handle our expertise. The more experience we have, the more we trust our quick judgment calls on increasingly fewer facts. Those calls can be spot on. An expert intuition is, after all, the benefit of years of hard work. But fast calls on few facts can prematurely halt investigative efforts. We stop looking because *"We know how this one goes, right guys?"* and risk missing key pieces of information that when raised by others will turn our persuasive narrative into a work of fiction. We need to hold off on being right long enough to prove it. Finally, do not stress if your theme is two or three words. Start with a paragraph if you need to. Begin by condensing your theme to an elevator speech—a presentation of your idea given in the amount of time it takes to ride in an elevator.[41] Then spend a decade or two learning how to get off the elevator sooner.

Perspective and Structure

1. The Expand and Contract Methods

Once we have the theme, we need to frame it and our logically consistent facts within a structure. The structure is never a prefab; we should always design it to fit each new story event. If, for example, we think that a big screen epic way of narrating is too confusing and unfocused for our report, we can create a narrow shotgun shack cottage, hoping to funnel everyone's attention through to the facts that matter most. If such a confined view of events would destroy perspective, then we expand the construct to a McMansion where everything we see as relevant can fit inside. When answering the Civil War question (referenced in the Foreword), Robert Warren Penn expanded his framework into a Frank Lloyd Wright prairie style design with its elongated and open flows. Rather than try to find one or two instances of glory during the actual fight, Penn telescoped his narrative shape to include the 100 years after the Civil War. It worked logically because he had been asked to explain present day attachments to that earlier conflict. In this respect, we are like architects, shaping the framework to fit our story's needs. Create an addition, if we need more breathing space. Erase the garage, if we, metaphorically speaking, cycle to work. If we know our audience hates condominiums, we do not rush in with a tube full of drawings filled with multiple unit and common grounds strategies, no matter how clever.

Perhaps what we really need is a patio. United States Magistrate Doyle Rowland once said to me, "Footnotes are a waste of time. If it is not important enough to put it in the body, then don't bother putting it in at all."[42] I rarely need a shovel in the face more than twice to learn what a boss wants, and have worked ever since to avoid the written aside. If I am convinced that I need to include a stray fact, but I am concerned that equally weighted treatment of it may give the reader a false expectation of my theme or ultimate reasoning, then I expand my narrative blueprint with discreet courtyards and balconies—small architectural above ground additions—rather than demote a particular subplot to a footnote. In my house plans, I never draw a cellar.

2. The *Rashomon* Effect

In Akira Kurosawa's film *Rashomon*,[43] four people witness a crime. During the trial, the witnesses describe the event in self-serving, contradictory ways. Yet as the bandit, the dead Samurai, the Samurai's wife, and a woodsman each provides his or her individual account, we accept that each one is true. Each recollection is plausible in a "Yes, I can see that it might have happened that way" way. There is a part of our brain that says, "Well obviously only one set of facts led up to the crime," while another part understands that reality is based on perspective. As narrators, our job is to uncover facts and work to set those facts into a perspective that appears the most plausible, all the while knowing that "the most plausible" is a matter of perspective.

Fortunately, we do not need heinous crimes and world class directors to remind us to respect perspective. A good story teller can help us remember. A Swedish friend of mine invited me to lunch and shared the story of her visit to China. She was one of a group of teachers who spent a week living in the Hunan countryside as guests of local farming families. One by one the colleagues in her group fell ill and returned to the city until she was the sole guest left at the home of an old, widowed farmer. He spoke only his dialect, which she did not understand.

On her second to last night at his cottage, my friend walked outside to brush her teeth. As she raised the brush to her lips, she noticed the brilliance of the stars in the sky and became so overwhelmed by the night view that she quietly began to sing, "Blinka, lilla stjärna där" ("Twinkle, Twinkle, Little Star"). The farmer joined her under the night sky and softly began to sing too, joining her in the same song in old Xian.

I could offer nothing more in response than a slight gasp, amazed at what she had said, before I began to wonder, "How could such a little song travel so far, and what did the boat look like that carried it?" Then my brain began to calculate all the other events that had to fall into place for this magical moment to happen: her journey there, the illness of her fellow travelers, the going outside to brush, the night sky, the spark of a thought to sing, her openness to actually sing, his knowledge of the same song, and his inclination to join her. All of these factors played a part. I held my breath for two seconds more as my skin goose-bumped. Then I smiled. That was one good story, I thought, but she was not done.

The next evening, the two sat for her final dinner. The farmer stared at the meager bowl of rice he had to offer his guest. Then he looked at his dog, and directed his thumb towards the pet. My friend shook her head, pointed to the bowl of rice, patted her stomach, and grinned. The farmer had wanted to offer her a more special meal of dog meat, as a way of honoring her. She found a way of communicating, "Oh, no thank you! I am so totally okay with the rice."

Goose bumps were now gone. The story suddenly swerved off course. My friend had done such an excellent job of recreating the scene that I was there in the cottage with the two of them, no, all three. I could see how the man and the woman sat on the floor with their bowls of rice, with the dog curled up somewhere alongside. I had gone so far as to imagine what I would have done had I been there in her place. I know me. I can be so afraid of offending or looking stupid that I will agree with someone even if I have no idea what they are saying. What if I had been sitting there, thinking that the man wanted to know if I liked his dog, or if I minded if the little fellow was there in the room with us while we ate? What if then I decided to simply nod and smile, and in so doing, suggest, "Why yes. I have a keen desire for canine. Can you recommend a good wine to complement breast of Fido?" Then the next sounds on the farm would be a yelp, an ax chop, and then a complete absence of diplomatic composure on my part. I went so far in my wanderings to consider whether I would cry. My friend's six or seven story sentences sent me off in a free association panic that was light years away from sparkling teeth and shining stars. Then I told her what I had been thinking.

"Oh, no," she said. "There was no way I would want to eat that dog. He had one eye bulging out and who knows what else was wrong with him." I was instantly off in another direction. Now I was out of the cottage and stuck with Santa's Little Helper, the family dog from the *Simpson's,* in my head. Only now Santa's Little Helper looked like he had been exposed to Springfield's nuclear power plant radioactive sharing, a-plenty. There I sat in an outdoor café in Malmö, my head leaning over a plate of sushi, trying to add a bulging eye to the familiar cartoon mutt, when I hit a tunnel. A darker process took over. I was not happy with my friend. *That* was her reaction? She cared more about genetically modified food than an eternal "Thumb's down. You die," for the pet? Fortunately I knew I was wrong before I could be stupid out loud. If I had been there, I would have had the same reaction. A strong visual could transform any pet into a disease vessel, especially if one has seen all one's colleagues fall ill. I remembered to consider her perspective. Her perspective was geographically and temporally relevant. She had been there when it happened. Her perspective, not mine, ruled. At the end of our lunch I asked my friend if she would go back to Hunan. "Go anywhere, actually," I begged. I would pay her to travel. The woman is a story magnet.

The "Swedish Teacher and the Hunan Farmer" story underscores that we need to be aware not just of perspective, but of its source: bias. I have not given bias a separate section in this chapter or any other chapter because bias cannot be compartmentalized. Bias is a lifesaver or a noose. I shared my biases—my immediate, uncontrolled reactions to every aspect of the story—to demonstrate that this is what a grouping of facts can do. Whether made up of three words or seventy sentences, a story event creates a reaction. But not everyone will experience the same response. How many others heard, as I did, the ax fall? Who else conjured up an animated dog from a television series, or became upset and then awakened? As we review information and work to coordinate it into an account of events, we have to ask:

What assumptions am I making and are they reasonable?

How will my audience likely react to what I am writing, and will that reaction be consistent with my assessment of the information?

We can never be certain of the answers to these questions. We are not even always aware of our own biases. What we can be, however, is mindful of the fact that the bias issue is big and must be constantly considered. In a perfect Word world, a bias check-off box would pop up alongside every paragraph of fact text we draft, but that still would not result in certainty. So we learn to depend on the story principles discussed throughout this book, from shift to perspective, word choice to theme, with the aim of channeling our audience towards a particular understanding of circumstances. We use several devices to move them towards goose bumps—or none.

3. Structure and Story Order

Each profession and field has its own operating procedures for gathering facts, but regardless of method used, I recommend a "more is more better" research mindset. Go for a larger sampling, a longer time, or a wider range. For years I have handed out John McPhee's *Annals of a Former World*[44] to my crushes, like normal people might make a mix tape or younger ones a playlist. The book is hardly the literary version of a Sam Cooke meets Adele compilation. It is a comprehensive survey of North American geology. But I want to share the beauty and magic. McPhee gives us layered detail from enough points of view that I believe everything he writes, even when I have no idea what he is talking about. His style had always been enough for me, but then it got better. I learned that his first job was in a lab killing fruit flies after experiments were over. (*A realist.*) He did not spend his high school years dreaming of the next best way to describe "rustling leaves." (*No drama.*) He reckoned he would end up in sports, until one miserably cold football game he ventured into the warm press box and decided that cold was overrated. (*Practical.*) When he did begin writing, he created a formula. (*Excessively practical.*) In an article in *The New Yorker*,[45] McPhee shared three methods for gathering facts, which I have tried to recreate:

ABD/C

How he applied these formulas, I understand, but they are not my point. That he felt compelled to *work* with formulas is what matters to me. It is geeky and wonderful, and comforting.

Once he has his facts, McPhee decides on a structure. On this he explained, "Structure is not a template. It's not a cookie cutter. It's something that arises organically from the material once you have it."[46] Narrators have several issues to deal with when evaluating a story structure, including plot form (classical, minimalist, or surreal), story elements (beginning, inciting event, resolution, and ending), number of story lines (single or multiple), point of view (first person internal or third person external), and time (chronological or flashback). Attention to these options will improve an audience's focus and interest in our business reports. For example, many of us can get stuck in a real-time delivery mode and write everything in chronological order. McPhee shows us that we non-fiction business writers have time sequencing options:

> *"It's the story of a journey. Within that journey certain things happened, such as an encounter with a big grizzly. That grizzly encounter was a pretty exciting thing, and it happened near the beginning of the trip. That was somewhat inconvenient structurally, because it's such a climactic event. But you can't move that bear, because this is a piece of nonfiction writing.*
>
> *"But what if you started telling the piece of writing further down the river, I wondered. That way, when you get to the end of the trip, you're really only halfway through the story. What you do then is switch to the past tense, creating a flashback, and you back up and start your trip over again. By the time you get to that bear, that bear is at the perfect place for a climax."[47]*

We business writers have the same options. We even have bears, although our grizzlies are camouflaged to look more mundane, like cracked pvc pipes or a claims file.

Where McPhee talks about structure in terms of organic flow, I envision architectural drawings to find my perspective and bearings. Each of us finds our own analogy, but as soon as I saw McPhee's formulas, I knew why his work spoke to me. Nothing about him is in the ether. He seems practical. No rustling leaves just for the sake of rustling leaves. He wrote an entire book on oranges, and titled it *Oranges*[48] Even the Pulitzer award committee agrees with me that he is a writer worthy of admiration. Yet it was the formulaic side of him that explained everything. We had to be related I began thinking, putting down the magazine, barely remembering Trillin's name.

Exercise #2. The Derby

Consider this hypothetical fact pattern. A football/soccer match between two rivals has the local stadium packed and frenzied. The visitor team just scored, and is in the lead. Sixty seconds after the goal, a home fan throws a firecracker towards the visiting team's goal and the visiting team's goalie. The firecracker explodes. Next we see the goalie walk away from his position, holding his ear. He continues to walk until he goes down on his knees, still holding his ear. During the distraction created by the explosion, a home team spectator jumps over the dividing board, and walks out on the pitch. The busy security forces do not see him. The spectator walks up to the goalie and shoves him. Security catches up with the spectator and takes him away. After both teams leave the field, officials end the match, handing a default victory to the visiting team. People talk about charging the spectator for contributing to the cancellation of the match.

What Mr. Spock and Donald Duck Have in Common

The assignment: write a fact pattern that defends the goalie-shoving guy. Begin with an out of time sequence and end with later determined facts that support the impression you are trying to make. Show remorse over the spectator's actions (because there really is no excuse for what he did), then head directly into a slow motion recitation of the events involving the noise bomb. Offer a physical description of the area of the stadium where the noise bomb was thrown. Call it a "bomb." Describe the type of seating, the type of fan, and overall crowd activity at the time the bomb was thrown. State the obvious, that the person who threw the bomb was surrounded by other people, other people who had an opportunity to see the bomb thrown. (We cannot say for certain who saw what, but there is nothing argumentative with stating that people had an *opportunity* to see the bomb being thrown.) Estimate the distance from the general area of the crowd to the goal, and do the same with the goalie with respect to his goal. Try to create an image of the commotion and frenzy in the end zone, and then launch into a description of the bomb: the noise, the flash of light, reverberation from the noise. Relate the sound to other sounds, like a gunshot, a canon, a jet engine ("one witness described it like the attack of a gunshot, mixed with the high pitch of a plane on a runway"). Suspend time. Focus on behavior.

> *"The spectator was on the pitch without permission. No one questioned him as he walked up to the goalie and with his four fingers shoved the player's shoulder. Security was too busy handling the events that had just unfolded seconds before. Someone had thrown a bomb onto the pitch. The explosion made the crowd freeze. All singing and chanting stopped. People gasped and bodies became rigid*

in reaction to the unknown. Then heads began to turn, as people connected the bomb with the now noticeable bizarre behavior of the visiting team goalie. The goalie, the opponent's star defender, had been on the pitch near his goal, but was now moving up the field, holding his ear and swaying about with zigzagging steps, away from the crowd behind him, away from the area where the bomb had exploded. His head was bent forward and he continued to cup his right ear with his right hand. His right shoulder was elevated and his face muscles clenched, suggesting discomfort or pain.

"The goalie no longer watched any of the action down field. He instead continued moving further away from his position. His unusual behavior drew the attention of his teammates, who likewise abandoned their positions and ran to his assistance. Either too distraught or in too much pain to continue on his feet, the goalie dropped to his knees, his glove still covering his ear and now cradling part of his face. He kept his eyes closed, as his manager dispatched the medical team. They began to rush to his side. The doctors would later explain that the bomb had caused serious damage to the downed goalie's ear. The goalie would not play the next two matches."

"What spectator?" is the reaction you want a passage like this to evoke. A shove? After 140 decibels explode near the goalie's head, directed at him from hooligans who protected the identity of the bomber and prevented security from being able to remove the offending spectator (and thereby the threat of another bomb), are we seriously being asked to believe that this match was shut down because of a four-finger push from an overly-beered eighteen year-old old lacking the premeditation skills of a streaker?

Now write an account that makes the man's actions seem as equally responsible for the end of play as the explosion and player injury. No argument, no opinions, and no derogatory words. Use only facts and perceptions, something like this:

> "The firecracker had gone off. All the security personnel in the area shifted down towards the noise. Their eyes shifted too, scanning the stands for clues. Security also needed to make sure other noisemakers weren't being lit, and to assure themselves that no one in the stands had been hurt. As John Smith, head of security, noted after the game, 'Our primary objectives were to prevent any other similar disturbances and make sure everyone was okay.' The spectator sat unnoticed. This was an important match. His team had lost the two matches before, and they were now down a goal just fifteen minutes in. He sat in the third row, as he always did, chanting the rallying cries and singing the game songs with the rest of the club supporters. But his blood alcohol level was at .19%, and nothing was between him and the now staggering goalie.

> "He moved down the stadium aisle steps, and vaulted over the almost two meter high stadium barrier to the pitch. He landed within the section of the field where security usually stands, then began to walk towards the goalie. The goalie was moving away from his goal, holding his head. The spectator continued advancing, this time onto the pitch, moving steadily with a determined stride the ten meters he had to cover to get to the goalie. As the spectator marched

on, the goalie went down on his knees, and closed his eyes. The spectator did not hesitate, did not change course, did not stop. Instead, he continued moving towards the injured and now downed opponent. The player's teammates were beginning to circle in, and still the spectator advanced. Then ignoring one teammate's plea to leave the injured player alone, the spectator reached out, pushed forward, and shoved the goalie. After this show of aggression towards the injured player, the goalie's teammates grabbed the spectator and took him to the ground. It took ten police to get the spectator off of the pitch. No one could be sure what would happen next."

Firecrackers go off on occasion and overzealous fans do manage to touch the turf, but for these random events to happen so close in time and with such frightening levels of animus and disregard, no manager would ever say, "Let's warm up our back-up goalie. We have the situation under control." This second account suggests that fault for the stoppage of the game lies with both the spectator and the bomb.

This exercise can be done with any dispute or event as a jumping off point for creating the strongest narrative possible for each perspective.[49] We can always find practice material, whether from news events, a bus stop conversation, or a child's dinnertime story about the recess bully. Increase your comfort by choosing an episode or debate within your profession or field. It does not have to be written, either. If you hear a story on the radio or a podcast, you can script it out in your head while you drive, sit, or walk.

Another plus is that we will not freeze at the thought of having to make things up. No one mistakes me for Hans Christian Andersen or Danielle Steele. Whenever any of my daughters ask me for a bed time story, I panic. I can field questions from judges in the highest court in New York, then go home and stammer at the prospect of having to create bedtime plot lines about the miniature dancing bear colony's adventures with the princess fish. I am, as perhaps it is with many of you, more comfortable working with tangible facts and real circumstances. This exercise is designed to practice new writing techniques by using existing facts as a jumping off point.

This is also a solid introduction to crossover. This is where it all happens. We can get good at recognizing patterning. We can pick the perfect theme and frame our structure to an engineered precision, but our facts will not persuade or compel until we learn the art of crossover. We need to move from dry, technical recitation to nuanced captivation. We do this by exercising a give and take between between communicative and expressive words and structures. If it helps to think of it in terms of split-brain analysis, we need to combine our left brain training and strengths and learn to develop, trust, and borrow from the creative right hemisphere.[50] Crossover is tedious and difficult to master, and punishing to your reputation if executed poorly. But mastery of crossover sets the writer apart and above. Exercises like "The Derby" help push our brains from settling in with a given set of facts towards a willingness to create a larger scene.

Larger scene creation can solve many business problems. Situations in life almost always have a hidden fact that either nags at our subconscious (the "something is not right here" reaction), or supports a perspective that we were too one-sided or tunnel-visioned to consider (the "Well, obviously, the situation is clear," jinx). To train ourselves to avoid this type of mistake, we exercise our minds to create larger scenes. As we expand the scene in our mind, we begin to get a grasp on what other types of facts we will need. Once big, we then work to restructure that scene down to opposing or alternate perspectives. As we narrow into alternate perspectives, we begin to see that there may be other facts we have not yet uncovered for these new angles to make sense. If our work requires us to support one perspective over another, then we know what we need to look harder for to support our position. We also understand better what to expect in opposition.

It is not just a "Go big then go small" task. We have to channel Helen Hayes and engage all of our senses. As sketched out the Derby exercise, I placed myself in the middle of an imaginary pitch and began to take in the scene. I heard the crowd. I saw the smoke as it curled around the end zone spectators and goal. I felt ear pain. I saw the tendons pop on the neck of the spectator. I watched management and players milling about inside the locker area, as they were waiting for a decision on the game. It was quiet for a locker room area, I thought, and most heads are bent in frustration. Men were walking without any real place to go. I went there in my imagination. This is even easier to do in our business writing because we are often completely at home with the subject matter and nature of events. Nothing is foreign and unimaginable.

Then rather than pick one side of the dispute, I work both, constructing two versions of events. Once I feel certain that I am seeing this event in a global and then narrow manner, and from different perspectives, can I then try to write about it. I use only facts. I never argue or suggest that the reader has to agree with me. I write it so my audience can also see, feel, hear, smell, or taste the facts as I am, because I want my reader to go there, too. I need to get the readers into the locker room with me if I am to have any chance of winning.

Chapter 3
Seeing Words Again for the First Time

Imagine trying to live in a world dominated by dihydrogen oxide, a compound that has no taste or smell and is so variable in its properties that it is generally benign but at other times swiftly lethal. Depending on its state, it can scald you or freeze you. In the presence of certain organic molecules it can form carbonic acids so nasty that they can strip the leaves from trees and eat the faces off statuary. In bulk, when agitated, it can strike with a fury that no human edifice could withstand. Even for those who have learned to live with it, it is an often murderous substance. We call it water.[51]

The strength of Bill Bryson's paragraph is in what he does not do. He avoids a deadly duo: emotive arrogance and beige staging. He creates interest and builds to a climax resolving into a shift, and he does it without an intolerant attitude or meaningless words. We follow him into the "Water, *of course!*" moment because his language is controlled and credible. We are moved without feeling shoved. "Generally benign," "swiftly lethal," "scald," "freeze," "in the presence of certain organic molecules," and "in bulk, when agitated," are words and phrases that maintain a scientific tone. He saves the least dispassionate descriptor, "murderous substance," for the last clue, when readers may have already solved his riddle. Most importantly, he did not use any of the following:

> *very*
> *interesting*
> *very interesting*

If the only step you take after reading this book is to remove "interesting" from your vocabulary, you will have advanced past 80% of business writers and 100% of all podcasters.

Bad Word Categories

1. The Panderer

Imagine this: You are standing at Point 0 on a decision line. An author of a business report chooses words he hopes will move you in one direction on that line. For example, movement towards +1 on that line has you inclined to approve funding. Movement towards -1 means no funding. You stand at 0, prepared to hear facts, including calculated projections, but the speaker ends with, *"The results were interesting."* What can you think? Nothing. Where do you move? Nowhere. You were prepared to hear facts that trigger a shift, but you heard only "interesting" and could not budge. Did the report mean interesting good, interesting bad, interesting big, or interesting small? We never find out.

"Interesting" is worse than an empty or weak word because it disappoints attentive listeners. The audience is left feeling abandoned on a subway platform waiting for a train that never arrives. The audience has not been told a thing. "Interesting" is at best a fence-riding, non-committal word. The writer wishes to avoid being specific in a business world where being specific matters. "Interesting" is at worst a lazy word. The speaker does not bother finding descriptors that explain why a result was unanticipated or beyond a norm. You should never use this word unless you explain immediately why the findings were so very, very interesting, or you are in the diplomatic corps.

2. Beige Staging

Aside from "interesting," I provide no list of words to avoid. Word-choice changeover is a gradual process. After we learn to drop the "interesting" habit, we can start identifying our most faded beige words, those bland, weak modifiers that invite an audience into a coma. Then we slate those words for execution. We begin to introduce memory words instead.

A memory word triggers sensory recognition in your audience. Sports fans can taste a reference to chicken wing sauce. Musicians' ears can conjure up a tuba quartet. We have all felt nauseous. Every baby boomer child who struggled to find a father's day gift remembers the scent of 70's men's cologne. Rainmakers see the shade *putting green* green. The beauty of memory words, however, is their success rate even when they are subtle. Words like bitter, chlorine, anxious, clang, and pale can be used in business writing and earn trophies when pitted against beige words like bad, odd, strong, regular, different, and good.

Each of us should be writing for trophies. Unfortunately, we hold back. We use beige words for a reason: safety. We are protecting our employed necks. Loss aversion is a strong motivating force; we have inside us a bias that favors maintaining the status quo.[52] We do not want to lose our jobs, nor do we wish to put at risk our team or company's bottom line. Safe words satisfy an internal survival mechanism. As Muhtar Kent, CEO of Coca-Cola, candidly admits, he has to be careful about the words he chooses. He must speak in a more general, less-direct way than he did before getting the nod to head the soft drink empire, a lesson he learned the first day of his job.[53] He has learned well. I have listened to his interviews and I am never sure enough of what he is saying to be able to comment. But Muhtar Kent has to be a diplomat. He is the King of Coca-Cola, and ambassador is part of his job description. It has never been a part of one of *my* job descriptions. My employers and clients want detail and specifics. They want less but more, fewer words and more insight. I could give them platitudes and boilerplate, but in doing that I only survive. If I want to move ahead, I cannot be bland. I must speak directly and in a way that captures interest. Memory words can motivate an audience, and sometimes that audience is a boss.

The hosts of *A Way with Words,*[54] Martha Barnette and Grant Barrett described the effect of semantic bleaching, words losing their brightness and vitality over time. We need to learn to spot this and let go of those words. With memory words we can make an impact. We trigger recall. When we write out the facts of an event, we use descriptive words that allow us to see, smell, taste, feel, or hear. To enliven, we use rhetorical devices like analogies ("The team began blowing past cost buffers like a hijacked commuter train"), onomatopoeias ("The bang from the gon dumpers did not exceed safety decibel levels"), or eponyms ("She's the Steve Jobs of the group"). Better still, we do not have to remember what these rhetorical devices are called.

I recently found Robert A. Harris' *Handbook of Rhetorical Devices*[55] and decided to read through his examples with the same dread and necessity that students look for posted test results. I felt a rush of relief. For every creative method I had learned to fit into a fact statement over the years, Harris gave me a respected name. I had not screwed up. I could have, easily, though. I had purposefully stayed away from instruction on rhetoric. I spent many years winging it because the examples offered in the how-to manuals seemed too strong and intimidating. If my reports began to read as if Winston Churchill and Oscar Wilde were helping me with my homework, I would end up demoted two floors down to the "What do we do with these employees?" section of the office. For many of us, sounding grand and important is never a writing option.

I avoided the "how to" and taught myself to bring readers in with simple descriptive phrases and wider, calmer perspectives. I actually remember the first time I dropped the "and" from a three word series in a legal brief. I would let myself break grammar rules if the error made the sentence boom like a canon and I was certain the audience would accept that I had intended it for impact. Harris helped me see that all this fits into what the old boys had already begun to categorize back when the word "rhetoric" was first uttered and togas were *the* fashion statement. I finally got to the creative writer's party, but I entered through the side door, quietly. For those of us busy with business, the side door may be the best way in. Do not worry about labels, avoid a template mentality, and remember that no matter what language each of us speaks, none of us has to learn a new dead one. We use what we know and tweak words and phrases over time. This helps us express our ideas more concretely with clients, teams and employers. They all "see" better what we are saying, but we remain employed during the process.

3. Jargon

Speaking of cost buffers...

> *"Failure was not invented here, yet our numbers make us look totally acluistic. We need a game-changing paradigm shift, and we all know that nothing major happens without sweat equity and traction. We need to drill down and focus on our SWOT analysis, leverage our core competencies, and pump up our best practices protocols, and we need to do it across the piece, now."*

Jargon has a bad reputation. Sometimes that reputation is deserved. Do your nerves cringe when the office sycophant says "assignment capsules" instead of "tasks"? If your new boss warns, "Your number one priority is base-tending," do you know in what filing cabinet or conference room they keep the "base"? Jargon can be phony and vague. It can a large sandwich board advertisement slung over your shoulders that says you, the presenter, are insecure and resorting to slick-speak to avoid concrete examples that you cannot handle.

Jargon can also be efficient. It can be the best way to communicate with your peers when time and energy is limited. If I am in a conference room with four of my colleagues, we will all know the short-cut language appropriate for a particular project. We will use it to communicate nuance and save time so we can quickly move on to the fact-specific details for which there are no shortcuts. If a friend says, "I have a beauty contest tomorrow," I know to wish him good luck and leave him alone so he can focus on selling himself to a potential new client. If I am on the phone with a customer, and we have been sharing the same fieldwork long enough, we can use acronyms and abbreviated phrases and feel good about how in sync we are. Every profession has its jargon. We depend upon it. Sometimes companies have their own dialect.

Problems arise, however, when there is a mixed audience, the term sounds forced, or jargon is used to replace critical substance. Fortunately, there are remedies. When communicating to a mixed room, I try to remember to ask myself if the insider argot I want to use is universally understood. If I am uncertain, I may still use the jargon, but I will add a follow-up phrase or sentence used to define or clarify the word or concept. For example,

> *"John had a reputation in the company as a brand terrorist. He seemed absolutely determined to destroy the business."*

If I did not know what a brand terrorist was before, I should now understand that BT is short for internal sabotage.

If I were Q and you were James Bond, I would hand over The Follow-Up to you with this instruction:

> *"Now pay attention, 007. This is the most important weapon at your disposal. Learn how to use it."* [56]

The Follow-Up allows the writer to shine amongst her co-workers as an expert, without risking jealousy. The Follow-Up is positive and egalitarian; it brings everyone into the fold and raises competencies. The Follow-Up never gets boring. If done well, no one even knows what you, the writer, just did, which encourages self-improvement in our competitive selves. All of these things together make it a secret weapon.

I spent many years working around others with impressive vocabularies and even more impressive IQs, and each new matter our group had to handle involved different technologies and professions. Everything that all of these people had to say was important, so the risk was always the same: will others understand the message? These brilliant folks would use their words and terminology. Thrown into the mix like a regression-to-the-means catalyst, I was there to try to figure out what they were talking about, and then translate. I learned to do it in a non-Oxford Dictionary way.

The Follow-Up is not just a device for translating the works of eggheads and experts. The Follow-Up is all around us. For example, masterfully done Follow-Ups can turn a television pilot into an Emmy award winning ratings-machine (another duality). Writers can appeal to a demographic that includes not only people who limit themselves to Scrabble, but also those whose joiner-talents are exclusive to beer pong. No one is left behind. Everyone has or gets a clue. The writers for the *30 Rock* television series geniused the Follow-Up. In this scene, the character Jack is explaining to his underlings why he was beating them in poker:

> Jack: *"See, in poker, as in business, the key to success is to determine your opponent's strength and, more importantly, his weaknesses. Everyone has a 'tell,' a weakness of character that manifests itself physically. …When Frank is bluffing, he asks a series of inane questions to hide his nervousness."*
>
> Frank: *"Oh, really? Is that what you think? Is that what I do? Am I doing that right now? Yeah, I'm out."*[57]

Actually, these writers worked in two Follow-Ups. The first was Jack's definition of the word "tell." He used a jargon term and immediately defined it. The second Follow-Up defined the word "inane." It is exactly the type of word that the Jack character would use. A part of the audience *needs* Jack to use words like that to accept the Jack character as credible. Another part of the audience, quite possibly the group that champions Frank, may not hear "inane" enough to know what it means. But another dictionary definition would be a bad plan. Defining an industry term is enlightening for an audience. Defining an unfamiliar word can be insulting. Frank defines the word for us by uttering on cue a series of senseless, empty sentences. The writers gave us examples of "inane" in context.

Another jargon by-product is hollow-speak. Hollow-speak is too many j-words at once. If we are listening to a paragraph full of it, we will not hear any message. To avoid these traps, use only one buzzword or phrase per paragraph or report, depending on how jargon-dependent the industry or profession is. Also remember that some of our verbal short-cuts are better than others. Use only those that produce imagery. For example, I am never going to say "facipulate" (to facilitate and manipulate at the same time). When I hear that word I begin to see a collection of letters unhappily mashed together. With something like, *"We have a longstanding policy on company romance: don't mess with payroll,"* however, I see co-workers transformed into deposit slips, and I smile every time.

4. Emotional Words

Calvin: "I've been reading about the beginning of the universe. They call it 'The Big Bang.' Isn't it weird how scientists can imagine all the matter of the universe exploding out of a dot smaller than the head of a pin, but they can't come up with a more evocative name for it than 'The Big Bang'? That's the whole problem with science. You've got a bunch of empiricists trying to describe things of unimaginable wonder."

Hobbes: "What would you call the creation of the universe?"

Calvin: "The Horrendous Space Kablooie."[58]

In his description of water, Bryson did not avoid the emotive. Bryson used words such as dominated, nasty, strike, and murderous. These words have a negative connotation and provoke an emotional reaction within the reader. "Murderous" is even an impossibility. Water may cause people to drown, but murder requires an element of intent. Water is not thinking so much about the type of carnage it causes. I used the Bryson example to show that in context and with proper timing, emotive seems less so. This is good to know. In the English language there are probably only seven words that are truly neutral. I have no idea what they are. I do not care. I prefer to work within statistical realities, and most things, including words, are relative. "Big Bang" may be less provocative than "Horrendous Kablooie," but only by degrees. What Bryson avoids is the *jarring* emotive, the sloppy adjective that tips a hand too soon and makes the author appear arrogant. As technical writers, we do not put judgment into our fact narrative. If we see judgment words too soon, most of us react by moving in the opposite direction. We do not have a choice. Our objective nature forces us to.

We know these value-laden words the minute we see them inserted too early in an article or report, words like:

Ridiculous
Obviously
Impossible
Simple
Clearly

I have never used "ridiculous" in a fact narration, and as soon as I insist something is "simple," my most important reader will furrow her eyebrows in disagreement. Based on her own experience, she will have recognized a complicated twist within my fact pattern. I will, in turn, look the idiot.

To learn what words not to use, we open our ears. Spend 48 hours listening to how people talk to each other. Ignore the actual sentence. Focus on each word at a time in isolation, and identify those that incite a reaction, even the smallest emotional wave within. Certain words will affect our heart rhythm, trigger our fight or flight impulses, or make us cringe. We are exposed to them in greater force and repetition now in arenas where objectivity once championed. As news shows continue to move towards entertainment, we hear more words that bully, mock, and harrumph. Journalistic integrity had kept these words at bay. Now, they enjoy command performances. In a world of reality TV programming, people seem incapable of forming an opinion without expressing it. Opinions are full of strong emotive phrases. Of this familiarity bred from exposure, we must be wary. Before we can begin to accept Dr. Frank Luntz's message, "It's not what you say, it's what people hear,"[59] we need to stop spinning long enough to learn what we, as people, hear.

When we take the time to listen for overly emotional words and phrases, it is easier to catch them as they come out of our own mouths or off our fingertips. Arrogant, judgmental words and phrases do not belong in fact narrations, even in those reports where analysis and judgment is expected. I may be called upon to report my opinion as to whether the actions of a team were a mistake. Whether something was an error or a mistake can be a fact. This is different than saying what they did was a *foolish* mistake or an *unthinkable* error. To protect our business or industry, we must be the watchdog and protect against the use of inflammatory and potentially damaging story adjectives.

With overly emotive words, a speaker tries to spoon-feed the audience. Our work is different. Business audiences are not babies. We have to build up a foundation with our facts, creating a platform on which the audience can stand. Then from that vantage point, the audience can look in the direction that we, at a later stage, recommend. I need story principles to get me to climb up on someone's presentation platform. I am not climbing up anything if what I hear in my first few steps assumes my position on an issue, especially if I disagree with that issue. Facts peppered with attitude, arrogance, and premature judgment only work if the audience is already on the platform and eager to look in the right direction. If that is the case, however, we fact narrators have no work to do at all. For that, all the company needs are cue cards, or a monkey. The future does not lie with primates. The future lies with those who can use story principles to overcome confirmation bias—the tendency we have to favor information that agrees with what we already believe. For over two decades, Gareth Morgan has been educating the business world on how metaphors can overcome confirmation bias,[60] and business listened.[61] Metaphors are just a small part of story principles.

5. Paper Clichés

Clichés are used for the very reason they can be a problem, they are familiar and clear. Phrases like "for all we know," "sight unseen," and "easier said than done" are a variety of beige staging and like a verbal tick they become a habit. The cliché gets its own category, however, because its risk reaches beyond bland. It can damage a reputation. Great communicators create phrases that become clichés. Poor communicators use them long after everyone else has stopped. The half-life of a clever phrase is about three weeks. After that, we need to create our own.

There are other problems with clichés. They time lock. If you explained that you stopped to take a photo because it was a "Kodak moment," will anyone in the office understand what you mean? Kodak became a film dinosaur in a world turning digital.

As noted by cliché-watcher, Alan Eggleston, "The danger with this [Kodak] idiom is that with the demise of Kodak, the 'Kodak moment' may now slip into obscurity or fall into a sense of the no-longer relevant."[62] Then there is the translation issue. Clichés can be local. Hearing the translation of "apples to oranges" into Swedish takes a few more seconds of conceptualization downtime because Swedes say "apples to pears." None of us is stupid. We will all get there. We will all eventually swap pears and oranges for oranges and pears, but not without the loss of what we were striving for in the first place: clarity and efficiency.

Word Comparisons

"Underpants" is a funny word to me. Maybe it is the American *a* sound in *paaants* that does it. In an empirical study of one, zygomatic muscles engage more with nasally sounding *aay* words. I smile when I say the word, and it somehow connects with the concept of happy. The same with the *ee* sound. Perhaps the physiological aspect of pronunciation makes the speaker and the language-familiar listener more receptive to silly. Less common sounds like the double *o* in *moose* and *pooch* and consonant combinations like the *p* and *nk* in *pink* also pack more humor potential than the common sounds in *dog* and *red*. I suspect that I am not alone in my appreciation of *underpants,* either. Sure, the subject matter helps. All body-related words that make seven year-olds shoot milk from the nose will continue to trigger the inner idiot, but sound matters, too. The children's series *Captain Underpants*[63] must have more pre-pubescent appeal than anything titled *Captain Underwear.*

"Underwear," in comparison, is as utilitarian a word as it is a utilitarian device. The word is dry and straightforward. Your audience is not likely to travel far off message. "Panties," however, is more difficult to gauge. With "panties," the listener has options. You may have just exercised one. We cannot be certain where the audience will go. The word can have one meaning for a man in that awkward stage between almost sophisticated and 107, while for a gaggle of "Gosh, I hope we can all be super friends" girls who are happy to introduce you to their roommate, Heff, it may *be* the generic word. "What's underwear?" the girls may ask. Although I stick by my statement that no word beyond "interesting" is off limits, we must still think: Which word should I use knowing what I do about (1) the story I need to tell and (2) the audience about to hear it.

Some languages have more word options than others. Some industries use a closed vocabulary. Each language and each profession has nuance, connotation, and phonetics in word choice. To help get comfortable with word analysis, turn to a thesaurus. Pick a word at random. Find the synonyms, and judge their impact. Arrange them in a chart.

Light	Generic	Erudite	Exotic
Underpants	Underwear	Undergarment	Panties
Noodle/Coconut	Head	Pate/Cranium	Skull
Sure	Certain	Convinced	Cocksure
Daily	Paper	Journal	Rag
Loopy	Drunk	Inebriated	Tipsy

Wheels	Car	Vehicle	Ride
Wacky	Odd/Strange	Peculiar	Weird
Picture	Movie	Cinema	Flick

Most light words do not belong in business writing, but we can add an underpants word on occasion to move the audience into a more receptive frame of mind. The words in the exotic column are generally provocative, titillating, street worthy, or vulgar, and—for the right audience—often overlap with light, funny words. These are great words. Learn them. Then learn to use them with caution. They can be effective tools in creating a shift.

> *"In 2007, we tried to incorporate patterns into our men's briefs line. Buyers responded as if we had offered them panties. Sales figures were dismal."*

Brainy, stuffy words in the Erudite column are creepers. Because of the company we keep and our need for various forms of continuing education, we are constantly adding more—and more difficult—words into our vocabulary. This is never a bad thing, but there are unfortunate consequences of educated people working closely together, including a loss of perspective on how gifted and talented each is. The "norm" is the norm of a highly specialized subset of people. Ironically, as we acquire more information through our specialized fields, we forget how specialized we are. We begin to think, "If I know this word, then everyone else must, too." Do your self-esteem a favor. Push the midlife insecurity-anxiety drama off a decade or two by reminding yourself, "I am smart." Then, return to the task at hand. Be smart enough to communicate well with the rest of the world.

On the other hand, we do not want to talk to people in a too-smart way. It is not nice, it is painfully obvious, and it is bad for business. For the same reasons, we never want to take our message and dumb it down. We must find workable communication zones. Imagine a globe, if it helps, and place your message's degree of difficulty somewhere between the Tropic of Cancer and Tropic of Capricorn. I also suggest never saying "vehicle" when you are thinking "car" (unless you are police officer), never say "prior" when what you mean is "before" (even if you are a police officer), and avoid all "hences," "wherefores," and anything Latin or more recently foreign. This is a start.

Exercise #3. Digital Visualization

How do we see the words we use? I see my words as components of block segments within the sentences I construct. At least I think I do. *If* that is how I see them, I am never certain if how I see them is right or wrong for persuasive appeal. I also lose objectivity. Our sentences become our children, and our children can seem so perfect at times. Then I wonder. Am I giving enough credit to repetition, emotion, and cadence? Because of these concerns, I have learned to cross-check my writing in other ways. One of these ways is dissection.

I selected my paragraph on 007 and ran it through IBM's Many Eye's data visualization program to create a tag cloud.[64] This is what the program returned to me:

007 attention bond boring brings co-workers
competencies competitive disposal egalitarian
encourages expert fold **follow-up** hand
important instruction james jealousy learn make
pay positive raises risking secret self-improvement
shine things top weapon writer

The larger the font, the more often I used the word. All words are in alphabetical order. The two-color system in the original Many Eyes program image is designed to help distinguish one word from the next.

What does my 007 reconstruction tell me? For starters, I had better be happy with "follow-up" as my central theme. I am. I also need to make sure my message survives negative words like "jealousy," "weapon," and "boring." I think so, but if I have any doubts, I can run my copy by those in the company with a better sense of word psychology and impact. Even without access to a program such as this, we can evaluate our word choice. We count up the working words and make a list, like this:

follow-up
weapon writer
attention bond boring brings co-workers, competencies competitive disposal egalitarian encourages expert fold hand important instruction James jealousy learn make pay positive Q raises risking secret self-improvement shine things top

The most effective use of dissection is in comparing an original text with an edited version. Take the original text and, using the dissection method, identify negative or weak words. Then rewrite the text. Run the two versions through the Many Eyes or the list process together. See how the word-use compares.

What amazed me the most the first time I tried this process was that nothing looked like mine. Nothing looked as I expected. By turning a paragraph of sentences into a list, we will see words that we did not realize we used. Words that fail to impact on us when read in context may seem larger when set apart in a list. Negative words can jump out, while our favorite nice and supportive words may weaken and pale. Words we use in phrases get torn apart. Separated, each word might survive or fail. Out of their sentences, words can have a different life.

"How did you get in here?" I think when I look at some of my words in the list. "Have we met before?"

Chapter 4
John Adams Was Right

A couple wishing to have their wedding announcement in the *New York Times* informed the newspaper that the groom's grandfather, Lord Harold Samuel, originated the famous quote, "There are three things that matter in property: location, location, location." Britain's *Sunday Times*, the *Financial Times*, and *The Daily Telegraph* all agreed that the quote was Lord Samuel's. The *New York Times*' Rosalie Radomsky and her editor, Bob Woletz, decided to dig deeper, handing the fact to be checked to the late "On Language" columnist William Saffire.

Saffire first approached the *The Yale Book of Quotations*,[65] which attributed the phrase to a 1956 article in a California newspaper. Saffire then queried another source, his wife's sister. Her late husband had been Lord Samuel's cousin. The sister found a contact, an associate of Lord Samuel's who was "90% certain" that Harold had used the phrase but would not commit on the point of origin. Saffire decided to call *The Yale Book of Quotation's* editor to ask if anything new been found. There had been. A 1926 real estate ad in the *Chicago Tribune*, read, "Attention salesmen, sales managers: location, location, location, close to Rogers Park." In 1926, Lord Samuel would have been 14, too young to be the source for the "location" quip, and, as Saffire noted, an unlikely subscriber to the *Trib. The New York Times* ran the wedding announcement without the reference to the famous phrase.[66]

The Times and *The Times* can debate whether the three words "location, location, location" was the sum and substance of the quote, or if, like Thomas Edison and the telephone, Lord Samuel should be credited with building something better out of parts that were already lying about not living up to their potential. I believe that Lord Samuel gave us something more. His addition of the word "matter" mattered. This is how perspective works. Yet the point that perhaps most truly matters in this story is the depth to which people will, should, and can go to uncover information. Here, the endeavor engaged one book, one computer update, five newspapers, six fact checkers, one witness willing to say, "I don't know," and math. With effort and candidness, a story acquires depth, and from that depth we as an audience can look with a perspective gained only through integrity.

John Adams knew. Facts *are* stubborn.[67] We cannot make them disappear with a clever phrase. We cannot argue a point as if facts do not exist. Like Taiwan, loud drunks, and *Times* etymologists, facts never give up. Facts demand attention. For this we eventually learn to be grateful. We need the *realness* of facts to act as stanchions and beams, markers we set throughout a story. As we desk-bound Tarzans learn to move from marker to marker, we change momentum and direction, and build interest. We decide where to place these markers—these facts—to create positive and negative value charge changes, and make our report feel structurally familiar, energetic, and credible. Despite these benefits, however, we seem to work to *avoid* facts. "Too many" facts will inevitably include too many bad ones. "Too many" facts will make things confusing. "Too many" facts is expensive. Time is money, and fact gathering takes time. Too few facts, however, is a death wish.

As a first year lawyer in a large law firm, I was one of many assigned to work with a particular senior partner. One day, he began calling, one-by-one, his charge associates into a conference room to ask questions about the lawsuits to which each was assigned. As I walked towards the conference room, another young lawyer was coming out of his meeting, shaking his head. "What a jerk," he was saying to his buddy. "I can't believe he expected me to tell him everything that was in those files." One part of me wanted to grab my colleague and strap a life-vest around him by warning, "No! That was a test and you just failed. You can't let it happen again." I had come to the firm after a two year appointment within the United States' federal court system where I had been trained to read every piece of paper in a file and consider its impact on a case. The senior partner was right, and I understood immediately that my co-employee would be gone by time of the firm's next holiday party. Another, controlling part of me allowed my legs to walk past the two, breathing a rare sigh of relief in those days, thinking only, "Today I will not die."

Gathering Facts

It might seem a basic concept, this need to hunt down and marshal facts. Yet we professionals, once familiar with a project begin to focus more on where we need to be and not enough on how to get there. We review a file with our sites beaded in on the most recent precedent, philosophy, or trends. Then we take the facts that best support our aim and jam them into our narrow field of vision. If instead we approach a file knowing that we will ultimately be setting up a story, we are in a better position to evaluate if we are seeing the matter from the most efficient perspective. Our fact narrative may allow for a broader, narrower, or additional legal principle, marketing strategy or financial approach to move us towards our target. Much of what follows in this section may be familiar, but even if you are brilliantly adept at fact gathering, we are working with a different filter now. If you have gone through the investigation process for a decade or three, you are now quietly reviewing information with movement, tempo, imagery, structure, genre, and impact in mind. Familiarity has moved you dangerously close to rote. You must know push as far away from data processing as possible.

Of course, to be able to work facts into a narrative, we have to actually possess those facts. Sometimes someone gives us everything we need to review. Other times, we start with nothing. Almost always, we do not have enough information and need more. We need to become skilled at getting more, which requires us to interview, observe, and research. To do this we must push away from the front of a computer screen and relocate our bodies elsewhere. We must interact with *humans*. We must ask questions on topics we do not know anything about. We must verify all that these humans tell us. To do this well, we have to risk looking stupid, feeling out of place, and being an annoyance. We must consider challenging protocols and established practices. Eleanor Roosevelt said, "Do one thing every day that scares you." We put our chances at having a full, satisfied life at risk when we hide within our comfort zone.[68] Fact gathering involves doing something scary, or at least discomforting, every day until the job is done. It is like going out for that cold, rainy morning run, asking someone out for a date, moving out of your parents' home, or asking your father if you can move back in. Before we begin, we don't want to, don't want to, *don't want to*. Doing this hard thing, the scary thing, or at least the uncomfortable thing at the office sets us apart. With enough tenacity and determination, it sets us apart in a good way.

"I never learn anything by talking." Lou Holtz.[69]

Once you have moved your body out into the public domain, you must arm yourself with ears, eyes, and an accident. Before you can become the great office storyteller, you will need to learn how to listen and observe, and then fall down the stairs. I am not being figurative, completely; I do not mean fail. I mean fall. Think about the last time you tripped across uneven concrete or slipped on ice. Time suspends when we fall. A split second of fumbling arms and legs feels like a minute as our brain calculates how to not end up on the down escalator with our skirt over our head. We can train our brains to suspend time like that when we gather facts. We learn to take information in as quickly as it comes at us, and then slow down enough to process what we have just learned. *Do we need to clarify a point and ask another question? Can he identify other sources of supporting data? She is avoiding the question. How can I ask it another way? What's going on here?* We do not go into a meeting with a list of questions and turn on a microphone. For that, we can send a robot. When fact gathering, we have to expect the unexpected. This only works if we focus intently on data in, and suspend time long enough to process that data before we next open our mouths.

All this must be done while developing trust with and applying insight towards our data source. When we seek information from employees, for example, we need cooperation. We need to break down barriers and open dialogues. We need to asses the credibility, motivation, and perspective of each individual we meet, from general manager to supervisor to clerk, and calculate whether and, if so, how the information each has provided needs to be verified. We want to protect each source, too. Unlike robots, we have souls. We also need to keep interviewees open to talking to us again later if we need more information. Eventually we evaluate how all the material fits together and assess whether some data seems missing or wrong. It may be easier to remember the following as "The *Who, What, Where, When, Why, How, and How Much?* Checklist," but I prefer to avoid the risk of oversimplification. I hesitate to even use the word "checklist" because it becomes more like a matrix that we constantly revisit and refine. We are about to meet an event, and our job is to reconstruct it in a *Rashomon* world. Better to think big.

1. No, *I* Invented the Internet.

The guest fell from the balcony and landed on the parking lot pavement, ten stories below.

John Adams Was Right

If I am a hotel worker who only observed the guest's body after the fall and included the above sentence in a preliminary report for my corporate risk manager, the seemingly straight-forward statement presents a problem: it presumes an answer to the *What happened?* question. I told my boss the guest "fell from the balcony." A person or body can *fall through* the air from the height of the balcony, a person can lose their balance and *fall off* of a balcony or lose their will to live and *jump from* or *jump off* a balcony, or a person can be *pushed from* or *thrown off* of a balcony. Each word combination sends a different message. Most of those require additional information. By stating "fell from the balcony," alone, however, the report unintentionally leans the story towards the accident. In a preliminary report it is better to state, "It appears that a guest fell through the air from an unverified height. The body has been identified as Lena Plume, registered to room 716. The emergency response team declared her dead. Room 716 has a balcony that overlooks the point of impact." We state just the facts. We draw no conclusions or offer suggestions at this time. This may seem unnecessarily rigid, but bear in mind that this is a fairly straightforward observation: one body, one sidewalk, an identification cross-check, and location points of reference. Now, imagine something more involved, something requiring a paragraph full of words describing drought projections or anything director James Cameron is engaged with at the moment, where there is zero tolerance for ambiguity. As we become more demanding of ourselves with basic fact reporting, we help guarantee a bullet proof presentation when working with more complicated reports, the kind of briefings that are less familiar to the public or more subject to peer review analysis. All of this brings me to my fast point:

Don't believe anything.

I am not saying people lie. People bring their own perspective to a story. They also bring their own word choice and sentence structure, and on certain days or projects or around certain co-workers, their own attitude. Rather than expect an absolute truth in anything we read, we learn to want to learn more than we are being told. This is a smart business approach to any fact investigation or review. Seek a better understanding of what has happened, is happening, and will likely happen within our system, program, or case. We may have six events contributing to one result, or one event causing six impacts. We should also consider any ripple effect from an action or an unconsidered cause. Maybe a fact looms large, but once we start digging we realize that it was never large enough to have been the catalyst for an event. Perhaps an event is barely noticeable, but like a rip tide, it has become the controlling undercurrent. We make notes of the seemingly small events. As we begin to develop a picture of what happened, we will make assumptions. These assumptions may be spot on, but we cannot let our expert judgment calls over-steer our investigative process. Sometimes small facts can have big impacts on a matter. Keeping track of them can help protect us from our own biases.

Gathering the *What happened?* facts is not easy. Every profession has its established methods, and these methods evolve over time. I offer six pieces of advice that work across processes. First, keep asking (at least to yourself) "what happened next?" Never assume a story is over. We never drop a story line because we think we are satisfied that we have heard enough, the speaker is finished, or the document trail is cold. There is almost always something more. Second, work to see the fact pattern unfold as a screenplay.

This process encourages us to remember to re-evaluate the *What happened?* issue within the added dimensions of *the who, when, where, etc.* questions. It reminds us to revisit and add to the matrix as our investigation advances. Third, run statistical probabilities whenever possible. What is the likelihood that something happened the way it is claimed? Statistical analysis can help protect against bias input from sources. As an investigation unfolds, our information will be obtained from individuals who have opinions and insight, memories, viewpoints, and perspectives (physical and philosophical). "Objective" is a more elusive concept than we understand, starting with a debate on what color is "red." Adding an element of mathematical probability to the storyline can help us assess the viability of what the experts, line managers, and bosses are telling us. Again, this is not a criticism of expertise or management. It is a safety net to protect us from our own egos. We all depend on our judgment biases, and they usually serve us well. They are not, however, infallible. Fourth, and equally scientific, find out what did not happen. Negatives are just as important as you learn about the event or the topic. Events that did not happen—events we would expect to see if another story line is to be believed—can become the most important facts in a matter. Writing a litany of bold negatives can have a dramatic impact in a fact statement. Fifth, find an expert. If the matter is complicated enough and we are doing a properly thorough job, at some point we will need help. We know when we hit critical mass. Experts help us identify what additional information to seek.

Finally, Advice Tip #1 has its limits. The better you get at this, the more you will want to dig. Unfortunately, few of us exist in a world of infinite resources. Accept that at some point in every matter, we have to let go. We have to work with what we have.

2. Location, Location, Location

We need to know all the places where events took place. We may need blueprints, zoning information, or photos. We want our audience to be in the room with us as we unfold our story event. This requires us to be able to describe that room, whether at an excavation site or office cubicle. It is not just the arena and atmosphere we want to see. People work at locations, and staff will tell you more when you are on their turf. Unless jammed into an interrogation room or threatened with job loss, employees at every level feel less intimidated and more inclined to prove to you how much they know, especially if you begin your interview with, "Can you help me understand?" Site visits are powerful story motivators. They help us write the "there" there, and gain leads.

Custom, dress, dialogue, doormen ... all these variables can play a part in a story, and often we do not realize they exist until we hit the floor running. Do the locals call the subway a subway or a train? Can you name drop the best BBQ stand in Dallas? Are you the only one on the sidewalk, the only one on a bicycle, the only one in a suit, the only one thirsty for a beer? In Casa Blanca, public concern leaves a trail like white chum from one stone-faced official to the next. In Charleston South Carolina, people use either "Piggly Wiggly" or "church" in every other sentence. That means something. Near the Sultan Mosque in Singapore you walk in off the orange, yellow, red, green streets into a stainless grey fish market and wait for bland-baited Midwest sinus cavities to explode with sea-bottom scents so powerful they trigger the flight or fight adrenal glands, then head to the nearest coffee shop, where co-workers with Pakistani, Indian, and English lineage laugh together over a malfunctioning cash register. Location experience gives us the insight on how not to be small-minded in our business reporting, what *not* to write in a report, how to leave our own baggage and parochial tendencies out of the picture. Most pragmatically, they help us see what the teller thinks but will never utter out loud. We can understand her better if we spend time in her environment. Even if none of these insights is keyboarded into a business report, they become part of our business acumen and certainly a part of our business communication skills. For this reason, too, it is worth getting away from in front of the desk and learning what there is to learn.

A location focus can serve a practical storytelling purpose, too. If we want to separate activities, such as making two incidents distinct and independent, then a geographical, physical divide works psychological wonders. Just as with The Derby exercise, do everything possible to create a West Coast – East Coast divide mentality, from weather to clothing color to vegetation and travel modalities. Reference time zones if they exist, and variations in office protocols. Physically separate the two operations, even if they are located at the same industrial park, using every image and concept tool available. If, conversely, we want to make everything and everyone tightly connected, then creating a sense of close proximity will better support our claim. Choose Example 2 over Example 1 to try to isolate a small group existing within a large community.

1. *Both women had offices in the Bank of America Plaza.*

2. *Lena's office was on the 51st floor of the Bank of America Plaza, and Amanda worked on the 49th. Both*

women entered the building through the same security check area, and used the same elevator group that services only floors 43-55. They used the tenant accessible only cafeteria, and both women belonged to the building's health club.

We are more efficient at this if we have been to the site or sites, but the location focus works even without the travel voucher.

This raises another practical point. Location visits are expensive. If we (1) identify them as part sales and marketing, graphics, research and development, and risk management departments' visits, (2) approach the visits as a reporter, (3) use and spread the gathered information with skill, and (4) maintain relationships with those we meet, we can demonstrate a solid value in the investment.

3. It Was a Dark and Stormy Night

In 1975 Jimmy Carter was a peanut farmer, Charlie's Angels was the most watched program on television, and the parties to this dispute entered into a partnership agreement.

Reports often begin with a date or time reference that adds nothing to the story value. Most of us would be better off beginning every report with, "It was a dark and stormy night," than by trying to encourage an audience to care with an opener such as, "The parties entered into a contract on June 7, 2004." Time matters, yes. We create a running timeline with each case as we investigate so we can find gaps and check relevancy. But using a date as the introduction should be reserved for intellectual property races and birthday party invitations, and even then only if done with spark. Dates are quiet, safe facts that we too often reach for like a security blanket. Unfortunately they almost always read that way. As with any fact, only reference those you want your audience using up valuable memory space remembering, and place boring but necessary facts anywhere but at the starting line.

When writing a report, we can structure with more staying power. We can choose a story order that sets out a separate line of chronological events for each dynastic player in the commercial enterprise, leading up to the current issue. Alternatively, or in some combination with this "chronology by customer," we could create a story order whose chronological order is sectioned off by location, by project, by disaster, by study, or—again—any combination of those types of subjects. One effective method is to use important date markers throughout. We build each party's activities up through to a certain date, note that date, and then continue on with individual party story lines until the next date marker. This can give the report a feeling of a race. Other methods include beginning with the recent past and then using subject matter-sectioned flashbacks to engage the audience. At the three-quarter mark of the report, wrap up the facts. Bring the reader up to speed and move on in a collective way from there.

We do not have to invent anything new. Story order options are all around us. From this point on, when you watch a movie or read *anything* that tells a story, no matter how short, look for a story order that you could use in your own type of work reporting. There are no rules, except to avoid confusion. Dates are markers that keep order clear, but as with the structural components of a building, try to find a way to keep these date markers out of sight. There is so much more compelling information for our senses to take in.

4. We Are All Spiderman

"Name me a reluctant hero, Syd," I asked my eleven year old, not expecting an answer.

"Spiderman," she said."

"You're right...How did you know that?"

"Because I know he didn't want to be Spiderman."

Every leading character in our story needs to have dimension, an internal conflict. Dimension has power. Eleven year olds understand this. They are not thrown off guard by someone's good grooming and a remarkable resume. They expect character development. Spongebob Squarepants has range. Yes, Sydney was right. Peter Parker did not want to be Spidey, and we thanked Stan Lee for Parker's internal conflict by keeping him Spiderman for five decades. Buffy was a reluctant vampire slayer. We adored her for this, and have welcomed hundreds of television vampires into our homes ever since. Macbeth experienced guilt. We adored him less, but we accepted his character. Without remorse, he would have been a killing machine and we would be crediting Shakespeare with originating the mechanical demon-slasher genre long before its time. Macbeth's sense of guilt made us believe that he was more than that. None of us is all good or all bad, or all right or all wrong. This truth applies in business, too. We gain credibility as narrators when we portray the subjects of our story with depth.

Who? can be the most enriching aspect of a story to develop, and it is critical to learn how to do it well. There are sound reasons for avoiding the all good or all evil character trap. Business leaders must make tough calls, but few decision-makers are eager to pull the trigger. If I want to wrest control of ABC Company from the founder and CEO, Adam Plume, I can write,

> *"Plume failed to introduce timely global marketing strategies and explore options to raise additional capital. Azon Company has collapsed under Plume's leadership."*

But then the board of directors has to be comfortable attacking Plume, a former hero, as inept. We can achieve our result by taking the time to at least recognize Plume's strength:

> *"We face increasing unemployment and inflation. We have also suffered the reduction of our traditional customer base. Our next concern is a severe creditor loss of confidence. Mr. Plume was instrumental in product innovation, certainly, but now global business conditions require leadership qualities distinct from his area of expertise. Discussions with investors indicate that we must engage in major restructuring, starting at the top level of management."*

Many might be quick to avoid this amount of detail, and dismiss these efforts as wasteful time spent on unnecessary PR or slick spin. "Never apologize, never explain," can be good advice. Before management decides how to publicize information, however, the information gathered should be thorough. These are facts. Facts give us the history we can reference to broaden the audience's knowledge, to give them a more accurate perspective on the sound rationale behind certain and often unpopular current activities. More detail requires us to conduct additional investigation, including interviews. This weaves us back to the point made in the *What happened?* section: Never accept without question everything we are told. We place ourselves in peril when we do that.

One does not have to change a sunny outlook on humankind, either—if such is one's tendency—to follow this advice. Even the most acclaimed can be victims of their own confirmation bias.[70] People assume. People believe. People guess. We all do it and I reckon (i.e. assume) that most people in business understand our only 99% standing in the perfection scale because I have never had difficulty asking my interviewees for back up documentation. "What you are telling me is important. I need to be certain that I can use it. What do you have that supports what you say?" Ask for other information—preferably documentation—as a cross check. If you are not sure you need more, ask yourself, "Am I comfortable telling my supervisor that I relied on this anecdotal information alone?"

In addition to having the capacity for assuming, believing, and guessing, people can also harbor unsupported opinions and self-motivating agendas. Remember how much we as a species work to avoid loss? When we are conducting an interview, we need to keep the interviewee's unspoken, constant concerns over job security and salary in mind. These reminders act as ballasts, helping us maintain equilibrium and stability as we work towards objective fact gathering. Staying mindful of reality, such as the power of loss aversion, keeps us from getting caught up in everyone else's drama. Drama exists in all professions, and at every level.

Finally, take a cue from Lord Samuel's associate. Remind others and yourself that the best answer is always the truth, especially when that truth is, "I don't know."

5. Say It Isn't So

Ask your interviewee how something happened, how a device is supposed to operate, how a prototype could be improved. The *How?* question may not seek or produce an answer as observable and seemingly objective as the "who, what, where, and when" inquiries, but we still need to know what those on the inside think. *How?* is also the natural lead into the important *Why?* question. The following interview is fictitious, but consistent with how some interviewees respond to questions. Individuals can be literal, nervous, protective of their companies, and upset with their companies—all at the same time. We have to learn to listen and ask the next question.

How was it to progress?

Ans. To arrive at point AF through point C.

Why was it to progress that way?

Ans. We needed that result in order to establish bond consistency.

How did it progress?

Ans. It got to point AF.

Did it get to Point AF through C?

Ans. No.

Why not? Was there a problem with bond consistency?

Ans. Engineering thinks it's a thermostat issue.

If the thermostat had been functioning properly, would you expect the readings to arrive at point AF through point C?

Ans. No.

Why not?

Ans. I didn't think we were running the correct compound ratios.

The *How?* questions give us a sense of the depth of a possible problem and lead to a *Why?* answer that may not be documented. This is especially true if your interviewees are problem solvers by nature or profession. They will want to help investigate.

6. Reason #38, What's Wrong With This Picture

Systems analysts may put little faith in the subjective *Why's?* in business, but this is a mistake. Opinion evidence is helpful for two reasons: We can make seemingly irrelevant information relevant and we open doors to higher levels. Getting in to see the boss is good. Sometimes, however, the only door open is to a mid-level employee. The mid-level offers you his opinion on the matter, sharing with you a bad fact. Once you corroborate that opinion, or at least the fact, with something from the documents room, you reach out to the head office. "It looks like things might not be exactly as we thought. Maybe we should meet to discuss this."

As for relevance, again we stop and think of the big picture. Not all information has to be objectively quantifiable to be probative of a business essential. If we go back to the "Point AF through C" questioning, the compound ratios might be completely accurate, but the researcher's opinion may bear weight on other problems within the system. We do not always use opinion evidence as truth of the opinion, but as evidence that someone within a company is questioning protocols, standards, or policies. This may be proof of a more systemic problem, and on that, the opinion bears weight. Only *Why?* questions and their answers get us this type of information. Importantly, we do not always need the answers. A fact statement can include a litany of possible reasons discovered during the investigation, and a litany of such possibilities can alter any dynamic.

I used to resist the *Why?* question because I never knew what the answer was going to be. I feared that once I asked the question, then any troublesome cat would be out of the proverbial bag. But only the *Why's?* allow us to most fully present the story of events. It is better to work with the cat, even a tiger, out of the bag then to pretend the troublesome feline does not exist. For story, there is a more compelling reason. The *Why's?* bring the depth to the story that fault brings to the depth of a character.

7. The Bottomless Line

The *How much?* question is where attention to the matrix and a separate notebook help maintain sanity. As we ask, "What happened?" we go back and forth to our matrix, exploring each person, each location, different time references, and different events. The money issue is no different than the rest of the inquiries, and as for all those columns of numbers, they are not enemy Roman legions. They are as approachable and workable as any other collection of facts we will face. Each principle in this book applies to accounting and finance as equally as it does to other professions and areas of inquiry. Some facts are hard and some are soft. Economics is actually called the soft science.

Equations may hold fast and theories may survive generations, but data is less secure. It is always subject to scrutiny. This is an area ripe for questions concerning what was not considered, not evaluated, or over valued. Omissions from and additions to calculations can be a big deal. Think less about challenging the equation, and more about reviewing the numbers being used in the equation. The values going in are almost always subject to scrutiny, and if we look for the story behind the numbers, then it can be easier to spot what is missing or off the mark. This is where fact gathering and the art of story can become the dismal science's best ally. As a profession with more unfortunate nicknames than annual Nobel prizes, economics can be intimidating. If it is not your field, breathe. There is a bigger malleable side of it all, full of personal, social, commercial, and political interests. So my best advice: when dealing with a numbers issue, hire an expert. My second best advice: even when no one is talking the bottom line, hire an expert. This is business. Money is always going to be a key driver.

Why Bad is Good

When presented a collection of facts, first try not to think too much beyond,

"What is in this mess?"

Do not worry about where you need to be, what the client needs, and whether the facts make sense. Review the materials. Then move on to step two:

"Do I see a story?"

Now remember you have a job to do. Based on that job, evaluate what you need to do with the facts. Where do you need to be? Third, stop and think one more time:

"How do I put this story together?

What is a logical, credible, engaging explanation of what has happened/is happening/is likely to happen?" To do this last part well, we must learn and grow comfortable with all the facts, good and bad. Only then can we can determine how to structure our article, brief, analysis, or report into that logical, credible, and engaging explanation.

1. Proper Sizing

There seems to be a pattern in life. Almost every matter has within it a good fact and a bad fact. If everything in a situation were all good or, conversely, all bad, there would not be much need for persuasion; we would be unanimous in our assessment and reaction, a less than regular event. Effective story narrative creates the best opportunity to acknowledge the bad and minimize its importance. Ignoring the bad only makes it louder and bigger when the opposition, competition, or regulator brings it to the audience's attention, as they certainly will.

The more information we have in our brains, the more options we have to write our fact presentations in ways that keeps unfavorable information in its proper perspective. We can use story principles to subtly demonstrate that the bad information is irrelevant, insignificant, fixable, or an anomaly, without our presentation sounding like argument. The same applies to a great fact—something colorful and revealing in our information folder that many might consider irrelevant—and we want to use this information without appearing opportunistic, or worse, desperate. Re-evaluate cause and effect, and expand the narrative. Make this fantastic fact intimately connected to the rest of the information and our theme. It can always be done.

2. Movement

His story *Complements* irritates me. I cannot shake it. Emile Zola wrote a short piece about a business plan: the sale of ugliness. A plain gal hires an ugly woman to be by her side in public.

> *"The monster alone on the avenue would have frightened you. The fairly good-looking young woman would have left you quite indifferent. But they were together, and the ugliness of the one heightened the beauty of the other."*[71]

My disapproval notwithstanding, the principle of contrast cannot be denied. "Good" looks better next to "bad." Bad gives us a chance to react up. From good, we can bend lower. From unfortunate events we can climb. "Last year was weak. This year shows stronger quarterly reports." "The future looks uncertain, so we are pushing our earnings as hard as possible now." The same applies to a character flaw, an unexpected test result, an opponent's success, or an ill advised move. We learn to treat these as complements that will, eventually, make us look more attractive.

Contrast delivers us movement. Author Kurt Vonnegut gave a chalkboard lecture on the shapes of stories. He made his shapes by graphing shifts in movement from ill fortune to good, which I have recreated here. He drew a two line graph. The vertical line factors graduate from unhappy (ill fortune) at the bottom, to happy (good fortune) at the top. The horizontal line across the middle marks the beginning of the story on the left and the end of the story on the right. He described three sample stories.

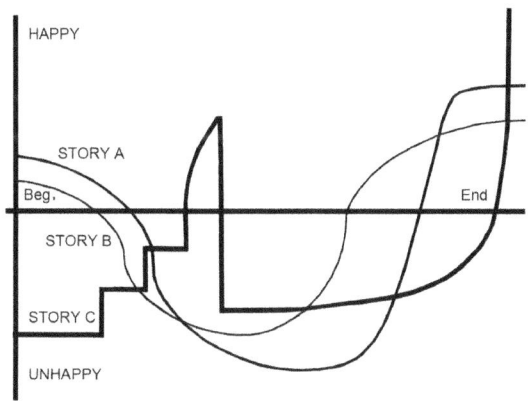

In Story B, the Basic, someone starts out in slightly better than average emotional condition, then gets into trouble, drops below the average happiness bar, and then gets out of it. "People love that story. They never get tired of it," he said. Story A, the thinnest line, is for love. Someone finds someone wonderful, so he starts out even more above average, but then he loses that love. His story curve crashes low below the happiness bar. Before the end, love returns and his line soars towards happy. Story C, the thickest curved line, is the Cinderella story. She starts out in the basement, and things begin to climb when she gets gifts from the fairy godmother. We know what happens after the clock strikes midnight, but because of the memory of the ball, she never drops as low as before. After the glass slipper event, the line rises to "happily ever after."[72]

It can help to conceptualize "movement" by drawing a horizontal line and moving a graph line above and below to reflect good facts and bad on your timeline. Most stories look more like mountain ranges and valleys. To gather and keep interest, we increase the height of the peaks and the depths of the valleys as the story progresses, with the most intense peaks appearing at the story climax, somewhere between the timeline's three-quarter mark to the end. Do not let the Cinderella fairy tale throw you off course. I include it to show that fiction (make believe) or non-fiction (what we do), the author has control over shape. Business events have movement, and a good story is nothing more than good and bad movement well tracked.

3. Handling Bias

Every audience has its own dislikes, leanings, opinions, and quirks. Every audience is unique. As these biases and attitudes surface throughout the life of a matter, we need to be able to handle them. For example, we may think we are on safe ground with our urban planning proposal, downplaying certain information because we brainstorm in a Chicago School of Economics philosophy, familiar territory for our city planners, only to learn that the new chief decision-maker is a Keynesian. More information gives us more options in preparing supporting data that will provide flexibility throughout all stages of a project. At some point in every matter you are handling, stop and remind yourself:

Always be prepared for the curveball.

Then dig deeper. While digging, remind yourself of this, too:

We can really never know anything with absolute certainty. None of us can, not even economists.

4. Patience

We should also work to follow the advice of the 1960's police character Joe Friday.[73] Every week on black and white TV screens he dispassionately instructed a collection of hapless, hysterical Los Angeles crime victims to give him, "Just the facts." This helps us learn to avoid all words and phrases that suggest a viewpoint or temperament. Facts gathered well help bring into focus a credible and logical account of things. People often turn to voicing disgust and waving arms to try to make a point. This is arguing, not fact reporting. Dealing with bad facts helps us learn to temper, to wait. The wisest piece of advice I ever received as a trial lawyer was to never let the jury see me angry until I knew that they were angry, too. Whether in the courtroom or the conference room, people need to be moved long before they get a sense that the speaker agrees with them. Towards that goal, nothing is more powerful than the combination of logic and credibility. Opinion in your favor should flow from momentum built by facts. Attitude alone never generates momentum. Attitude should never be first.

Story Structure and Logic in Action

Imagine an executive summary that seems to have all the parts. It begins with subject matter sentence. It discusses the methods of analysis, offers findings, draws a conclusion, makes recommendations, and mentions limitations. It reads something like this:

We have analyzed and evaluated the present and future profitability, liquidity, and financial stability of Azon, AB. We also calculated leverage (debt to asset) and liquidity (current and quick) ratios, rates of return on shareholder equity, and earnings and total assets per share.

We believe the ratios do not meet industry averages, especially with respect to credit control, liquidity, profit margin, and inventory management. The company's prospects are not positive. We believe that remedial action is needed in the following areas: increasing inventory, increasing sales, and reducing accounts receivables

There are several limitations with our investigation. We lack information on current economic conditions, including monthly details. Because we do not have this data we based our forecast on past performance only. We are also in need of general forecasting figures for this type and nature of company.

A report like this might meet executive summary standards, but there is a problem that someone with story skills can recognize. The drafter turned the executive summary into a mystery novel. *We have run extensive ratios. This company is in big, big trouble. Here are some problem areas that must be addressed immediately. Oh, and, by the way, none of our information is current or industry specific.*

The report uses strong language to mark the company as a fiscal train wreck about to happen. Then, at a point in the story where our brains are conditioned for a story climax—at or near the end, the drafter says, "Here is why we may not be correct." The author of that report told his audience to no longer trust the report. If those limitations are immaterial, meaning that the other available information is so troublesome that current data could never change any reasonable financial expert's mind, then the story solution is to mix those limitations in at an earlier point of the report:

> We reviewed Azon's records for the past five years and ran a variety of ratios, including leverage (debt to asset) and liquidity (current and quick). Although we were lacking current monthly details and forecasting figures for this type of company, we followed SAPs and analyzed rates of return on shareholder equity, and earnings and total assets per share. We are confident in our calculations and projections, copies of which are provided in the appendix.

Use conventional story order concepts to trigger fewer alarms. Here is another example of an executive report error:

> Azon has asked us to examine why the sales volume of Azon Cola has dropped in the past three years and whether there are any steps available to increase sales.

> Three years ago, Azon held 40% market share of a $50 million volume of cola sales. Babs Cola held 22% of the market, and Cricket Cola came in at 20% market share. During the past three years, the volume of cola shares has fallen to $38 million. Azon has held its 40% market share.

> Our research shows that the loss of sales volume overall is occurring as media and news are increasing discussions on

sugar intake and diabetes. At the same time, there is an increase in non-sugar drinks, including sugar free colas and specialty sports drinks. We believe that the new drinks are the reason for the $12 million reduction in sweetened cola sales.

Azon has recently developed a sugar free cola, using a sugar substitute that is free from the health adverse reports associated with the most commonly used sugar substitutes on the market today. We believe the sugar free drink would help increase sales volumes. We recommend launching the sugar free cola, placing the product in sports complexes and health stores, in addition to our traditional supermarkets.

Film studios hire continuity experts to make sure that after all the editing is done, the actors and the items within camera shot are the same from one frame to the next. A continuity expert catches and fixes the little things that change when actors have to go through several takes to get the scene right. For example, if a camera is shooting a couple sitting at in café, the continuity expert makes sure that no coffee cup disappears, or that no extra comes in and sits down at a table between takes. As viewers, we need the details to be correct, and this is just the visual aspect. The same applies to the actual story line. We need the logic flow.

This report fails the flow. For example, why mention the other two cola companies? There is no additional information that tells us what has happened with their market shares over time. I am left wasting precious corporate seconds wondering why they were mentioned. The other error places us into non-traditional sales locations. Nothing in the summary discusses research into point of sale data. We are being urged to make one of two changes—expanding a portion of a $12 million sales effort into a new point of sale location—without any reference to supporting information. If most of the sales continue to be at low overhead supermarket chains, then making a decision to service niche markets through vending and specialty shops requires a different analysis. In the first example, it is as if a coffee cup disappears from the table in the film shot. The other cola companies are there, but they then disappear without explanation. In the second example, the push to stock health stores, it is as if another body suddenly shows up at the table. "How did he get here and for what reason?" we wonder.

I modified both of these summary examples from reports that were given good grades by business reviewers for coherence and assembly. But "good enough" should not be good enough for any of us. Story structure, order, and patterns help us evaluate the strength of a report beyond an acceptable template, good grammar and correct business jargon. Story takes us to a higher standard, and helps us see how we can do better.

Exercise #4. Know the File

The Know the File exercise trains the brain to consider and filter a vast amount of information while making the brain's owner take a critical look at her skill level in narration. It is like the "current location" indicator on a GPS. Write two short autobiographies, both addressed to either your significant other or mom—two different tries, written to the same audience. You know all the data about the subject (you), and you understand your audience and the type of information with which they are comfortable. Put the bios away for a week, and then read them. Judge which one is better and try to figure out why. Do not show the intended recipient and ask what he or she thinks. This is not a time for criticism. In fact, destroy them.

Next, write two autobiographies in which you brag about yourself, almost the alter ego, pumping up with full bravado your accomplishments and conquests. Here your audience might be the friend who lived through some of your escapades with you, or someone you wish to impress with tales of your reckless abandon and nerve. This usually brings out different facts and a different tone and voice. Again, put both pieces away for a week, then review, chose, and erase.

Finally, write two autobiographies to yourself, describing successes, milestones, failures, and disappointments. Without using argumentative words or excuses, present the facts to justify anything negative in your past. Be honest, but always with a spin in your favor. You are the protagonist of this story, so write it that way. Wait to read. Then delete.

The exercise may seem unnecessarily extended, perhaps even light-minded to some, but if done in earnest, it produces six different story approaches concerning a lifetime of information that requires no down-time for research. Plus, it is all facts and no argument or plea, so by choosing different bits of information for different audiences, and working to expand upon or temper some parts of a personal history, the writer begins to see how narration can be used for subtle persuasion. Finally, waiting a week increases objectivity in your review. I am always impressed with what I write when I write it. At some point the next morning, I am hitting the delete key.

We can also consider this exercise conceptually. We think about writing the six bios, but never actually do it. For many, the point can be driven home to the ego without doing the work: *perhaps my writing skills could be better.* Before skipping the Know the File exercise, however, understand that developing one's art of story will take a long time and a library full of redrafts. A client or a boss may not be the best beneficiary of your first attempts. If you do this exercise, and at the end you are satisfied with your narrative persuasive skills, chose someone—intimate, cohort, or obituary page reader—and write one more short autobiography geared towards that person. Ask for an opinion. People may not be comfortable or familiar with editing, so be prepared to beg, but do not be embarrassed. When you ask someone for help, what they think is, "He knows I am so smart." Your smart reviewer will be honored that you have selected her to help you. Once in that feel good place, she will be more likely to focus on your draft, and voice honest reactions.

You can either rinse and repeat as necessary with you as the protagonist, or develop characterization by doing a similar exercise using a close family member or friend as your subject. Fictionalize it if you need filler. Then delete. **Delete.** No matter how proud you are of your final product, it will take another ten years before any family member will understand what you are trying to do.

Chapter 5
The Real Boss

Jack Kerouac had nothing on our group. We were not hoping to discover ourselves or any obscure truth. Drinking to the point of escape, although considered, was not an option. The most we hoped for was a chance to venture out and to return home intact. This was true road adventure, moms-stuck-with-kids-for-the-whole-weekend style. My friend and her son, along with me and my pre-teen daughters drove a long stretch of Ontario highway in search of Canada's version of a drive-thru McDonald's and Serengeti Plain mash-up. The big difference here was that any food that would be passing through a car window would be a body part belonging to one of our gang. "When will we get to lion safari?" my friend's two-year-old, John, kept asking. Sandwiched in the back seat between my own progeny, he spent the passing kilometers removing items of clothing and escaping his seat restraint. "John, it's time to put your pants on," my daughter Paige said when we finally saw the adventure park sign. She thought he would hear this as a happy *"Now! We are getting there right NOW!"* answer to his "When will we get to there?" loop. John, who had been straddling his booster wearing only a pair of XXS underpants and one shoe, heard it differently. Lions no longer roamed his imagination. He turned towards Paige in determined defiance.

"You are not the boss of me!"

My eyes connected with Paige's. Authority issues? Sure. We also knew that the kid had just delivered one fine—and to us then—new phrase. During the next 45 minutes we all repeated, "You are not the boss of us!" non-stop at the aggressive Canadian safari monkeys who sat on the car's hood, feasting on the windshield's rubber sealant that they had mistaken for a delicious licorice treat. The incorrigible primates had their own listening issues. We drove out of their electrified fenced-in area and into the man-eating lion-land with a sense of doomed *Jurassic Park* foreboding.

"My husband's going to kill me if that front window falls out," my friend muttered. "If this window falls out, your husband's going to have to take a number," I answered, spotting a lioness up ahead. As I read the situation, the felines were now in charge.

Knowing the Audience

1. New Journalists, Move Over

The audience is the boss of us, the person now in charge. As a concept, "audience" cannot be reduced any more than that. Sometimes the person who approves your raise is the audience. Sometimes a client is the audience. The audience can be the public, a competitor, colleagues, an administrative judge, or employee. Often one report will have multiple audiences. This complicates our lives, but it does not change the concept. The audience is the boss. Because of this, we have to know the audience.

This is not a new insight, this need to know. But saying, "Know your audience," feels as helpful an instruction as yelling to a three year old, "Hey, kid, tie your shoes!" Understanding how to know your audience takes practice and time. Other writing processes have gone through periods of evolution and come out ahead. During the 1960's something called New Journalism began showing up in newspapers. Certain reporters were challenging the tradition of writing based only on what the journalist saw from a distance. The reporters were learning how to get *inside* the subject matter:

> *"They had to gather all the material the conventional journalist was after—and then keep going. It seemed all-important to be there when dramatic scenes took place, to get the dialogue, the gestures, the facial expressions, the details of the environment. The idea was to give the full objective description, plus something that readers had always had to go to novels and short stories for: namely,*

the subjective or emotional life of the characters....The most important things one attempted in terms of technique depended upon a depth of information that had never been demanded in newspaper work. Only through the most searching forms of reporting was it possible, in non-fiction, to use whole scenes, extended dialogue, point-of-view, the interior monologue. Eventually I, and others, would be accused of 'entering people's minds' ... But exactly! I figured that was one more doorbell a reporter had to push."[74]

Today, all of us business writers, we non-fiction reporters, need to push another doorbell. If Wolfe and the other New Journalists improved their profession by getting inside the subject matter, we non-fiction writers need to push our skills by focusing on the reader. The concept of "audience" is in a phase of its own now. "What is inside the head of my audience?" we need to ask. Lots of things, is the answer, even with an audience of one. The difference for the New Journalists then and us now is the depth and breadth of our investigation. Superficial does not cut it. Only once we can sense the pulse and sweat of the audience, can we begin to edit.

We start with a single issue, as an example. If our job is to sell something the color orange, we need to know if our customer hates that hue. If he does, we must start with the understanding that we can never change his mind. We will never be able to convince him he is wrong. If we try to suggest that orange is a beautiful color, his ears will not hear our words. He will mentally if not physically dismiss us.

If, having done our homework, however, we learn that our customer is health-obsessed or style-trend conscious, we can discuss how people look healthier with a sunset glow bouncing off their skin or that Pantone just identified the color of the year as Tangerine Tango.[75] If one bias cuts us off, we look for other avenues. There is a longer-term benefit to finding ways around an audience bias, too. Here, for example, once our audience becomes comfortable with orange in his life, he has a hard time remembering that he ever hated orange in the first place.[76] Discussions over the color orange may seem superficial, but the same principle applies to bias in race, religion, sexual orientation, economic theory, brand allegiance, political persuasion, and whatever else we could face as a fixed, predetermined, intractable-seeming state of mind.

2. How Many Are You?

When fictional detective Sherlock Holmes claims that life is stranger and more fascinating than fiction, his collaborator Watson, disagrees:

> Watson: "And yet I am not convinced of it. …The cases which come to light in the papers are, as a rule, bald enough, and vulgar enough. We have in our police reports realism pushed to its extreme limits, and yet the result is, it must be confessed, neither fascinating nor artistic."

> Holmes: "A certain selection and discretion must be used in producing a realistic effect. …This is wanting in the police report, where more stress is laid, perhaps, upon the platitudes of the magistrate than upon the details, which to an observer contain the vital essence of the whole matter. Depend upon it, there is nothing so unnatural as the commonplace."[77]

The Real Boss

Holmes blames the police department's focus for the dull read. The officers are primarily interested in ingratiating themselves with the local judiciary. They are sucking-up to the magistrates, their audience. So rather than provide provocative information on the crime, the police spill their ink flattering judges. If crime solving were their major focus, then the police would have targeted the crime solving detectives as their audience, and the amount of detail would have been enough to show the truly bizarre nature of our very non-fiction, bad behavior. *Who* our audience is, alters the focus. It is a bigger shame that the police did not consider writing for both audiences. *How many?* is just as important a question as *Who?*

In my first jury trial, I defended a machine manufacturer whose equipment ripped the skin off a factory employee. The insurance company assigned to the claim had already put the law firm I was working for on notice that it was taking its future business to another firm. I had never seen the case before it landed on my desk a few weeks ahead of jury selection. Gossip suggested that no one wanted to risk a million-dollar career hit for a customer that had already said good-bye, so the firm tossed the case to a new kid. I was to going to have to cover this trial like a live grenade.

I had three audiences: a jury pool conditioned by events in the region to hand out big money to injured workers, a judge who would have to decide all legal issues, and the insurance company representative to whom I was to report daily. I knew four things. First, the jury would have zero tolerance for any suggestion that the injury was the employee's fault. Second, the machine manufacturer was at a disadvantage both because of its corporate status and because it was not a local company. Third, the judge had a reputation for being fair. Fourth, the insurance representative would not want to write out a big check, so he would be reasonable.

To handle the jury, I decided to expand the fact pattern. "Let's show them how good you are," I said to the client. We spent all of our prep time, the manufacturer's president and I, figuring out the best method for highlighting how many safety mechanisms were built into this machine, and how critical loss prevention was to the company. The worker was able to override a mechanism—something that a jury will punish a manufacturer for not preventing. Here, rather than talk about what the employee did, we focused on the sincerity and abundance of the manufacturer's efforts. The jury accepted our facts and decided in its favor.

It was a good thing that I was correct in my read on how the jury would react to certain key issues, because I had miscalculated the biases of the judge and insurance representative. In fact, I barely gave either of them any "audience" consideration. As the case and the strength of the company's position progressed, the judge began to make increased requests for me to offer a settlement to the injured worker. It made sense. As good as it feels to take a trial all the way to verdict and win, there is always a risk of loss, and a loss here would have been expensive. A small settlement would have been smart. I had been reporting daily, advising that the matter was going well, and asking, as the judge had instructed, for a settlement amount that reflected the risk. Yet the representative kept telling me to soldier on.

On the last day of proof, the injured man's lawyer asked the judge for permission to show the jury the photos of the injured man's body during surgery. The photos were inadmissible under the law, a point I had argued and won earlier in the case. But when the attorney repeated his request at the end of his proof, the judge turned to me and asked, "Do you have any money for settlement?"

"No, Your honor," I replied.

"Photos in," the judge ordered.

I felt sick. I had allowed myself to be blindsided. Perhaps I had been old-boy'd by a long-standing relationship between the judge and opposing counsel, or sucker-punched because the judge wanted the injured man to receive some money. One thing seemed certain: I had miscalculated the temperament of my audience the judge. I had been careless. After viewing the gruesome images, the jury still decided in the manufacturer's favor and the trial was over. My lesson in "knowing the audience," however, continued.

I said goodbye to the company president and walked back to the firm alone. Once in my office, I called the insurance company with the result. "Good," the representative said, "because I didn't tell you that I never had money set aside to settle this case, let alone pay for a verdict. And I'm surprised you won. Juries don't like female lawyers. I am *really* surprised you won."

Congratulations, I thought. I had taken two out of three audiences for granted. I had failed to foresee the representative's bias against women lawyers. I should have put that bias on my checklist and made a note to learn how to handle even the suspicion of it. I also should have taken the time to think about why I was not getting even a small bit of money to make the case go away (something almost always done in those days). Rather than communicate facts needed to get to a more responsive level of authority (the insurance company had money to pay the claim), or communicate some of these issues to the judge, I let my ego control. "I'm not getting money to settle because I am so good. The judge must be seeing how good I am, too. It is good to be so good."

It was like the thesaurus all over again. I had so much to learn.

Later, after I become a boss, I would realize that I had failed to properly analyze one more audience from that event: the firm. Customers are precious. In high risk lawsuits, clients want the top lawyers handling their matters in front of a jury. This means that it is a rare opportunity for a young lawyer to get needed experience taking a case to trial. A senior partner had directed the case to me so I would learn trial lessons others would have to wait a few years to get. I should have ignored the gossip and reported more openly to him, working to better analyze the judge's behavior and read what was going on at the insurance representative level. No matter how many are around us, when working on a company project, we are part of a much bigger team. The company is always one of our audiences.

3. Beyond Aristotle

We are not always aware of which bias is controlling. Some information is available through research. Judges write opinions, people belong to political parties, department heads issue memos, politicians offer interviews, and social media and co-workers "share." Yet often we learn of an audience bias in the middle of a presentation. What do we listen for?

I'm not seeing how this fits.
I don't understand.
We have budget issues.

The Real Boss

What else have you got for us?
I like it. Let's talk about it later.
Great initiative. We like to see that energy.
(Silence.)

Sometimes we get this notice early enough in the life of a project to give us time to come up with alternative narrations. When facing a one-shot opportunity, it helps to already have at least two issue-shifters built into the fact presentation. Here is an example.

If we think that video-medicine platforms are a critical part of medical practices in the future, then we need to present facts on the topic to our medical clinic's CEO. Our report will include information on technology, trend projections, cost benefit analysis, and licensing restrictions. We know that the licensing restrictions alone are insurmountable obstacles without a change in legislation. Because of this, we recommend that our company works to increase the medical professionals and legislators' familiarity on the topic by asking to be allowed to use our program for those in isolated areas or people otherwise segregated such as prison inmates or victims of natural disasters with limited resources, and only for treatments that do not always require physical examination, such as psychiatric care.

We should expect our CEO to be less than enthusiastic. She will probably feel that it is not worth the money, she does not want to jeopardize her relationship with the professional medical associations, she is not in the business of politics, she may not lose sleep over the condition of the prison inmate population, she knows a natural disaster has not hit Nebraska since, well, ever, and she will probably feel it is not worth the money.

We have done our homework and anticipate these concerns, which is why we have prepared the option of (shift 1) starting small. At this time, we only want to introduce the *concept* of telemedicine to our patients because at this time, the best we can hope for is (shift 2) a change in public opinion. Fortunately, such a change is exactly the kind of grass roots movement needed to make larger legislative amendments later. We also need to (shift 3) stay ahead of the curve on technological advancements of the practice of medicine. Everyone brags about having the latest MRI machine and the hottest new pharmaceuticals, but our doctors— and the doctors and medical professionals we want to attract— need to see that we are at least exploring much larger and lucrative private practice options. If we do not get started on this, our bigger concern (shift 4) is that we will actually lose our market advantage because we are known trend leaders.

We want our company to fund a major lobbying effort to make telemedicine happen. We want to get in on the beginning of what we believe to be a substantial part of any medical practice in the future. Knowing our audience, we narrow our focus and use loss aversion bias as our back-up for getting approval for a concept project. (We do this with facts, not argument as simplified here.) This is enough. We have gotten our big camel nose into the tent. Once the nose is in the tent, the rest of the camel will follow.

Bias is intimately connected with how an audience listens. Thomas P. Mullen and Mala Narrain of Park Li Group explain that members of an audience will focus on one of four primary elements: data, structure, vision, and the human element.[78] Because we cannot be certain how any particular member of our audience processes information, we need to create our narrative with every type in mind. This means that our story needs to have a solid foundation in facts and figures (data), an overall image of how all the information fits together (structure), a map of where we are going (vision), and a flow-chart of how everyone fits into the plan (the human element). We have been talking about these points throughout the book, but when presented in terms of how an audience member may listen, we see again why story principles belong in business writing. We need to gather facts, we need to frame a structure, we need to create movement, and we have to make every audience member envisions our message.

Editing

> *"I try to leave out the parts that people skip."* Elmore Leonard[79]

For some of us, editing is the communication part of communication. Writing is getting all the kids together on the practice field. Editing is turning those kids into a team. Editing is more than just the spell and grammar check on a software program. When it comes to storytelling and persuasive narration, there needs to be a structure check, a bias check, a logic check, a theme check, a word count check, a shift check, a clarity check, a tempo check, a bad word check, a sensory descriptor check, a reality check, and the rest.

The spellcheck is finite. The options we have for spelling "apple" are not so many. With grammar, at least tempo and style begin to surface. My grammar check will often suggest the active voice over a passive construction, even though there nothing technically incorrect with the passive format. I *prefer* the passive voice when I am missing facts, I am admitting to a bad fact, or I want to set a contrast. My grammar check yells at me when I create a new verb or drop a conjunction for emphasis. Like a harangued spouse, I have a passive aggressive relationship with most rules. I work with the following techniques instead.

1. Read Out Loud

Author John McPhee's father did this—read his papers out loud while editing. His dad was a doctor, not a novelist.[80] Every sentence has a rhythm within it, and every sentence creates a beat that introduces it to the next, but not all rhythms work. Not all beats segue smoothly into the next. When we read out loud, we improve our ability to hear this cadence.

> *"Writing prose without thinking about cadence is like trying to seduce a man by handing him your résumé. The facts are there, but the electric charge isn't."*[81]

Trained voices recite the Koran following "detailed rules for pronunciation, rhythm, and sectioning" to make it sound beautiful and help the listener understand and memorize.[82] These imprinting principles are universal, even when applied to small passages. Consider:

> *A job begun is half finished*
> *A job begun is half done*

We are more likely to remember the aphorism that rhymes.[83] On this point, however, we have to be careful. We are not in the habit of recording messianic messages or using rhyming words for our business reports. We should not be, either. We do not aim for "grand"—or immortality—in our progress reports. Our task is much simpler. Read everything you write out loud. If it sounds good to the ear, it will get into the brain.

2. Expose Yourself

Write or speak for an external audience. Create a blog or podcast under an assumed name. Propose a sports, music, or advice column under a pen name. Find the public outlet trending at the time, and write in another style on an almost daily basis. Even just the possibility of others seeing our efforts at an unfamiliar form of writing dramatically speeds up the learning curve.

I began to blog over ten years ago. I was reluctant. The few bloggers on the web back then read like underemployed men with overblown opinions. Yet I remember the afternoon I sat at my desk, looking at some papers I had written. They were not good enough. I had hit an impasse. My passion had always been to search for the new legal angle, but I found myself working in an area of practice where novelty was a decreasing option. When it came to creative argument, there was no more part of the envelope that I could push. To win, I would have to use only facts—and not always favorable facts—to persuade my audience. I would have to write in a way that made busy judges and their busier law clerks *want* to read my work. I knew the answer. My brain needed boot camp. Only instead of getting yelled at by drill sergeants, my training would have to be by something much more terrifying. I would force myself to post on the internet. I walked into the firm's open area. "Does anyone know how to blog?" I asked.

"I do," said the lawyer with the bow tie and an undergraduate degree in English lit.

"Of course," I sighed, hearing the clang of the boot camp gates close me in.

It worked, over time. I began writing columns for an award winning magazine, and I learned how to edit. I studied how to help the eye see more on a page and find ways to give dimension to the parties in a lawsuit. I began to build movement in a "[Insert Statement of Facts Here]" template. Then it happened. A prominent lawyer described my legal submission as the best mediation brief he had ever read. "What?" I thought. "*What?*" This man entertains diplomats and rock stars. My brief was about insurance contracts and airport security, hardly the stuff of screenplays. As I stood motionless, overwhelmed by his remark, it hit me. If I could do it, anyone could.

The thought went further. If someone was willing to give me a "best" award, then we as a profession were not pushing ourselves enough. It is understandable. Once on the hamster wheel, we rarely take the time to self-assess and retool. Going public is one solution. By going public, our learning curve becomes a trajectory, an extremely uncomfortable trajectory. Yet almost no exercise is more effective for critical self evaluation. Before we hit the "post" button, we ask, "Will anyone like this?" "Am I offending?" "Am I funny?" "Will they stick with me to the end?" "Have I minimized the risk of negative comments?" "Will people understand what I am saying?" Then it gets worse. After we hit the post button, we see it published. We will notice immediately how we could have done it better.

In your own company, work to build within everyone a tolerance for the red-line. Move people into a group mentality by creating editing cliques. This is "going public" in a different way. "I want to change how I write my reports. Do you mind giving me your feedback?" When you get your drafts returned in massive mark-up, do not argue. Study the changes. Process the other person's analysis. File that information away. Keep doing it. The group can be one trusted colleague or a collection of co-workers. Ask to review as much others' work as possible. Editing another's writing helps each of us eventually see our own style choices with better eyes.

3. Grammar

Whatever your language, do not break grammar rules for emphasis until you have proven that you know the rules in the first place. If you are not sure of the rules in the first place, keep your sentences simple. As we work to create compelling narrations, we cannot forget that some people in our audiences wear extremely tight grammarpants. Some of these very people may not stop to think that many of us may be writing in a second or third language. It is not their problem. It is ours. We cannot change a perfection bias. *We* have to adjust. My recommendation is to find the path of least resistance. Does the proper use of "whom" intimidate you? Then rewrite your sentence to get rid of it. Want to try to solve a grammar question, find your language's version of Mignon Fogerty's *Grammar Girl,*[84] and fill in the search box. Seek accessible, good-natured help. You are learning about humor and story principles. Grammar is important for clarity and persuasion, but what we are engaged in now is a new frontier. We need to stay focused and unintimidated.

Unintimidated remains key to the process. Unfortunately, grammar is a large lecture hall full of cruel professors. I counted over 100 comments in the online *Economist* "Language" column for a post on the use of a comma splice (the separation of two sentences by a comma instead of a period or semicolon). Yes, almost one hundred people took the time to weigh in on a punctuation form I did not even know existed. In the process, one of the commenters felt compelled to trash an innocent bystander, the semicolon, with a quote from Kurt Vonnegut's, *A Man Without a Country*:

> *"Here is a lesson in creative writing. First rule: Do not use semicolons. They are transvestite hermaphrodites representing absolutely nothing. All they do is show you've been to college."*[85]

Most of us have been to college. It is okay to use the semicolon. Vonnegut seemed more keenly focused on logic and the semantic relationship of the two then provocative words "transvestite" and "hermaphrodites." He was showing off, and the poor semicolon ended up collateral damage. Sometimes two sentences feel like a big brother and little brother standing next to each other. Each is his own person, but the two share a stronger relationship than the rest of the sentences in the paragraph. The two are linked. The semicolon gives me that link with *visual* cadence. Others may see this as structural balance. Writing is a visual medium and, yes, it is okay to have a brain. It is also okay to make mistakes. I am still learning, too. In time, however, we notice that if our narration is captivating enough, we can survive the cruel professors. We can even learn to enjoy the brilliant pontificators. Here is the good fact: There is always *someone* around on the office floor anxious to correct our grammar. Find them and learn to thank them. A technical writer with developed skills in wit and storytelling is rare. Becoming that person is *your* job. Stay focused on developing the skills that will set you apart.

4. Cut It Out

Sometimes my writing gets puffy. Pages fill up with comfort phrases like "and that which" or long, complicated sentences that run parallel with over-zealous mental processing. I would feel at the top of my game while my writing enters the snore zone. I put myself on a ten words per sentence diet whenever I am feeling too important. There are variations on this reduction plan. When Facebook's social networking site had a status update character limitation, I worked to condense an 800 character anecdote into half the space. Twitter's character limitation offers a greater challenge. Some of us think these exercises are fun. The rest of you normal folk do not have to agree, but try it once. That may be all it takes to spark your editing brain.

We can strive to avoid redundant words, weak modifiers, and verbal ticks. We can work to turn adjectives into verbs and general nouns into specific. We can promise ourselves to restrict the use of "which," "that," and "who." But do not create a list now. Options like these will start to surface with one thought: "Lose it."

5. Don't Cut Funny

If it is subtle and passes the review of two uptight co-workers, leave it in the report. Successful humor swings a very wide and favorable bias in your favor. Wit requires a clever brain. Never cut demonstrations of it from the final copy.

6. The Matching Game

Stories have plot-types and genres. Most audiences have a familiarity with the differences between the classical plot and the minimalist plot, and the action-adventure, detective, romance, tragedy, comedy, suspense or historical drama, and science fiction genres. If you are trying to sell a book or a screenplay, you will learn that the market has conventions associated with plots and genres, and that you will have an easier time selling your story if you follow those conventions. We are not using our business writing to get on the *New York Times Bestseller List* or red carpet, true, but we should never underestimate the power of the familiar. If our facts make us think of a particular plot or genre—if, for example, our story feels like it has all the makings of an action adventure—then we write it with a nod towards action genre conventions. Why? Convention helps the audience accept it. We are creatures of habit. If it sounds like a duck and walks like a duck, then success follows presenting it like a duck.

Plot, genre, characterization, and timing are all difficult concepts, especially when our focus is on business and technical writing. Our reports are short, but we should still keep plot and genre-related questions in the back of our minds. We get better with this over time. Over time we learn to ask, where do the shifts happen and how often, how does the suspense build, do our facts have a resolution, how does this all relate to our theme, what is the pace, or what is the focus—the characters or the scene? Is this a story that relates to mankind, or is it better for us if we isolate it into an individual? Do we have a protagonist, an antagonist, and any supporting characters, and if so, how have we worked them into the narration? Do we have a series of scenes with value charge changes that together result in a major shift within our company? Do we have an underdog or revenge issue, or are we looking at morals or public policy? Do we have a resolved ending or do we care only about a small part of a big picture? Is this a *Perfect Storm*[86] or a ship of fools? Is it personal, is it sad, has someone been educated, has someone been killed, is it political, or does it seem like a documentary? We get there, eventually. The only uncertainty is whether this process gives us the right to deduct as a business expense the price of every ticket to every movie we have seen the previous year.

I'm not kidding. Keep your receipts.

7. One Voice

On papers that take one employee days or weeks to prepare alone or with those reports authored by many working together, read the document through for consistency of voice. The final product should sound as if written by one person who is emotionally stable.

8. Statistics

I will be working with this issue in more detail in the next volume, but for now, consider options for cross-checking your story message against the biases that statistics show exist in your audience. Cross check your story message against the biases that statistics show exist in your audience. We cannot ever know how our audience will receive and react to our story. At best, we can make judgment calls based on our audience research and behavioral studies. Because we will always be uncertain, we need to begin trusting percentages. How, based on statistical analysis, can we best hope to move our audience? This is a new frontier and worth developing a comfort level with because it will become an increasingly powerful tool in the effort to manage bias.

Negotiators have used the anchoring effect for years to edge individuals in a dispute to a point of agreement. Anchoring is a tendency we all have to attach too heavily to one given fact. If I tell you that I think our neighbor is 50 years old, you will automatically move away from any thought you may have had that he was 35. Because I spoke first, you do not know his age, and you trust me, you will move your mental calculation over to where I dropped my fact "anchor." You may debate with me over whether or not our neighbor could be 40 or 45, but you will never mention 35. The anchor will not let you travel that far adrift, back down to 35. You will not want to appear clueless. If we know absolutely nothing about an issue, statistics prove that we are likely to go with whatever anchor we hear, regardless of how off-base it is in reality. The more we know about a topic, the more observation plays a role, but the actual anchor controls much more than our conceit allows us to believe.

We talk about anchors in stages of argument, but they also have a place in fact presentations. So does priming (conditioning the associative memory to respond a certain way), exposure effect (increasing memory association through familiarity), and confirmatory bias (our tendency to interpret information in a way consistent with preexisting beliefs). I earlier discussed memory bias and loss aversion principles, but there is much more in the field of cognitive biases and effects. All of it relates to the persuasive nature of story.

Because we can never really be certain how an audience will respond to a given collection of facts, we should not hesitate to return to logic. We may find an answer in how to best present our narrative to an unfamiliar audience by looking at statistical probabilities. Go with the numbers. As technical writers we are learning how to crossover into forms of creative expression. Once there, however, we can not forget that we constantly need to cross back.

Exercise #5. The Discomfort zone

The next time you are in an airport, go to a newsstand. Head to the magazine section. Walk away from your favorite publications. Buy a magazine on a topic you know nothing about. Better, buy a magazine on a topic you avoid. I discovered this exercise fifteen years ago, by picking up a copy of *The Economist.* "I'm going to learn this stuff," I said to the cashier. She nodded, "Next!"

My education into high finance quickly turned into a game. I started in the back, with the obituary, a full page spread of the only material I reckoned I could grasp. Then I began to read the glossy in reverse order, from the last article on through to the table of contents, quickly developing the game "Find the Gratuitous Jab Against America on Each Page." I soaked up the dry wit and respected the writers' skill at making complicated global finance issues almost comprehensible. I repeated the exercise with *Wired, ESPN*, and *Esquire* magazines. (I tried the *Journal of Foreign Affairs*, but I need pictures if I am going to stay awake.) I exposed myself to different writing styles for different audiences. I would also try to find the gaps, or calculate how, if the columnist had been writing to a broader audience, she would need to change the copy. Another benefit of this exercise is that each of us has an invaluable excuse for having whatever reading material ends up in our desks: "Leave me alone. It's for *work*."

Eventually you can expand the exercise into podcasts, but I recommend that you begin by reading. As with the first exercise,

"Finding Funny," our brains process in print better, at least initially, and the exercise transfers more efficiently because we are writers ourselves. At some point, our ears become equally receptive, even to air editing. One word of advice, keep a paper and pen handy for those names and phrases you hear and do not want to forget. And maybe keep that pen in a pocket protector, because, well, you know. We are who we are.

Conclusion

"Now I am going to tell you everything I know about penguins.

Penguins live in Antarctica where it is cold. They are birds. They eat fish.

That is everything I know about penguins!"

"What is this?" I asked my third grader, an impatient finger landing on the lower part of a page filled up in 72 font sized letters. "It's called a 'conclusion,' *Mom*," Haley replied. "It's what my teacher told me to do. A conclusion is supposed to say what I wrote about. I wrote everything I know about penguins."

I instructed my little *spheniscidae* scribe to educate the world a bit more on her subject matter, and then taped the rough draft to my office wall. "That is everything I know about penguins!" became in-house code for "not enough." I needed my own reminder on how to wrap a story. Perhaps it was even genetic. Introductions can be the the stuff of legend. Body content is my specialty. But conclusions? I always figured that if I have done a good job, then my audience should be all set and ready for action before the final pages. A conclusion is redundant.

"I got to the end of Chapter 5 and wanted to go on," my contributing editor said. "If you are ending this volume here, then at least give me a conclusion."

"That is everything I know about crossover?'" I said.

"Not enough," Lisa replied, her finger starting to twitch. "Not even true."

But a conclusion should not be much more. If the best piece of advice I ever got was to not let a jury see passion too soon, the second best piece of advice was to capture the audience early. Get the story image out while you still have interest. The big finish is a fiction. No argument, no pitch, no video is going to get you the grand prize if you wait until the very end to show it. It is better to feel like a barely-above the ground helium balloon by the time you type "Conclusion," than to be all ready to bust with excitement. In other words, be done. Your report, statement, analysis, or journal article must use story and humor principles of pattern, movement, tempo, structure, and order, from the beginning to the almost end climax to carry your audience past all the possible logjams that an opponent, circumstance, or third-grader can throw in your way.

Finally, whenever possible, use the end as an opportunity to swing the beginning around, so the audience is reminded of where they started.

> *Two polar bears, two penguins, and a dog with a bandaged front leg walk into the Fertile Crescent bar in Mesopotamia. The bartender says, "What is this, some kind of a joke?"*
>
> *The polar bears say, "We're looking for Nuh and his boat."*
>
> *The penguins say, "We're looking for Noah and his ark."*
>
> *The bartender turns to the dog and says, "Yeah, yeah... all this noise about a flood. What about you? Where's your mate?"*
>
> *"I don't know about them," the dog said, holding up his injured foot. "I'm just looking for the man who shot my paw."*

As a joke, the joke bombed. Half of the focus group stopped listening after the name "Nuh." "Don't you mean Noah?" Someone immediately corrected. No, I wanted to be more inclusive so I intentionally referenced the Muslim version of the flood. Then I had to explain the old pun, that anyone who has ever seen a western movie would understand that "paw" was a substitute for "Pa," meaning "Dad," and that they would instantly remember some random cowboy actor storming into a Hollywood-set saloon and telling the bartender that he was seeking revenge against the low-down dirty scoundrel who had "done his family wrong."

"What do the penguins and polar bears have to do with the dog?" another asked. "Look," I continued, annoyed. "You didn't even notice the classic bartender joke within the joke, 'What is this some kind of a joke?' and how after that I followed John Vorhaus' advice to create a gap—to cause the audience to expect one line of inquiry following the bit about arks and yachts and paired polar opposite animals, but deliver something altogether different. It's a funny joke, trust me."[87] But I know how it goes. No matter how much the visual absurdity of penguins alongside

an ornery dog with a great line slays me every time, a joke that has to be explained is not a joke at all.

But as a signature Full Circle, the joke bombed less. A Full Circle is a great tool, especially efficient when the story has traveled a long distance from its starting point. It reminds the audience of a lesson offered at the beginning of the adventure. There are many devices to find and explore as you work to incorporate story and humor principles into your writing, and the Noah-turned-Western bartender joke mash-up survives the final cut because it is one such device. I brought the dog back in, in the form of a weak joke, to remind us all of Lebowitz, Thurber, Barry, and Hayes and how masterfully they finessed Fido. Business is tough. When it comes to persuasive, engaging narrative writing, we can never stop striving to write better. Fortunately, non-fiction fact reporting in the business world is easy.

No, wait...

References

[1] Cleanth Brooks and Robert Penn Warren, *Fundamentals of Good Writing, a Handbook of Modern Rhetoric,* (New York: Harcourt Brace, 1950).

[2] "Nora Ephron, Adult, Revenge, Group Therapy and Pot Roast," *Academy of Achievement Interview,* http://www.achievement.org/autodoc/page/eph0int-5, last modified October 14, 2010.

[3] Ken Burns, et al., "Disunion: The Civil War," *Times Talks,* http://nytimes.whsites.net/timestalks/podcasts/, podcast 1688, April 8, 2011.

[4] Brooks and Warren, *Fundamentals,* http://www.archive.org/stream/fundamentalsofgo030292mbp/fundamentalsofgo030292mbp_djvu.txt, 3.

[5] D. Kumar, N. Ramakrishnan, M. Potts, and R.F. Helm, "Algorithms for Storytelling," IEEE Transactions on Knowledge and Data Engineering, Vol. 20, No. 6, pages 736–751, June 2008.

[6] Pam Belluck, "To Tug Hearts, Music Must First Tickle the Neurons," *The New York Times*, April 18, 2011, http://www.nytimes.com/2011/04/19/

[7] Robert Penn Warren, *The Legacy of the Civil War: Meditations on the Centennial*, (New York: Random House , 1961), *see also* David W. Blight, "150 years after Fort Sumter, forces that gave rise to the Civil War still plague modern America," *The Daily News,* April 12, 2011, http://articles.nydailynews.com/2011-04-12/news/29426649_1_civil-war-bruce-catton-oracle.

[8] *The Official Website Lou Gehrig*, http://www.lougehrig.com/about/speech.htm

[9] Anthony Bourdain, *Kitchen Confidential* (New York: Harper Collins 2000).

[10] *HBR Ideacast*, "Anthony Bourdain on Why Leaders Should Eat with the Locals," interviewed by Suzie Jackson, April 14, 2011, http://blogs.hbr.org/ideacast/2011/04/anthony-bourdain-on-why-leader.html

[11] Michael Quinion, *World Wide Words*, January 14, 2012. http://www.worldwidewords.org/weirdwords/ww-par5.htm

[12] Fran Lebowitz, *The Fran Lebowitz Reader,* (New York: Vintage Books, 1994), 242.

[13] Dave Barry, "The Importance Of Being Earnest If The Name's Not Lassie," *The Chicago Tribune*, September 29, 1985.

[14] CBS, *Lassie,* http://en.wikipedia.org/wiki/Lassie.

[15] Chris Columbus, Director, *Home Alone*, 1990.

[16] James Thurber, "Snap Shot of a Dog," *The Middle Aged Man on the Flying Trapeze* (London: Harper & Brothers, 1935).

[17] Helen Hayes, with Sandford Dody, *On Reflection: An Autobiography,* (Philadelphia: Lippincott, 1968), 198.

[18] Brad Anderson, *Marmaduke,* Universal Uclick.

[19] David Sedaris, *Me Talk Pretty One Day*, (Boston: Little, Brown and Company, 2000), 74.

[20] *The Bugle Podcast*, http://www.thebuglepodcast.com.

[21] Anthony Lane, "Euro Visions," *The New Yorker*, http://www.newyorker.com/arts/critics/cinema/2008/07/28/080728crci_cinema_lane?currentPage=all

[22] Stuart Miller, *Mark Twain, Essays and Sketches of Mark Twain,* (New York: Barnes & Noble Books, 1995), 71.

[23] Charles Dickens, *Little Dorrit*, 1855-1857. Project Guttenberg, July 1, 1997, http://www.gutenberg.org/ebooks/963

[24] "The Madoff Recovery Initiative," www.madoff.com.

[25] Catherine Berlin, "Size DD Brain, Please," *Buffalo Spree Magazine,* Vol. 42, November 2008, 87.

[26] Tina Fey, *Bossypants,* (New York: Hachette Audio, 2011), Audible.com edition.

[27] Gail Collins, "Unwelcome Surprises," *New York Times*, March 13, 2008.

[28] "The Sheriff of Wall Street," *60 Minutes,* CBS, Producer Trevor Nelson, Correspondent Steve Kroft, October 6, 2002, http://www.cbsnews.com/video/watch/?id=4501767n

[29] Nina Bernstein, "Foes of Sex Trade Are Stung by the Fall of an Ally," *The New York Times*, March 12, 2008.

[30] Andrew Leonard, "Eliot Spitzer's monumental fall from grace," *Salon.com*, March 10, 2009, http://www.salon.com/2008/03/10/spitzer_fall_from_grace/

[31] Helio Fred Garcia, "Humility Update: Elliot Spitzer, the Iraq War, and Lessons for Leaders," *Logos Institute*, March 17, 2008, http://logosinstitute.net/blog/2008/03/17/humility-update-elliot-spitzer-the-iraq-war-and-lessons-for-leaders/, and Steve Fishman, "The Steamroller in the Swamp, *New York Magazine*, July 23, 2007, http://nymag.com/news/features/34730/index8.html

[32] *Esquire, The Rules, a Man's Guide to Life*, (New York: Hearst Books, 2003), 52.

[33] Sarah Vowell, *Take the Cannoli* (New York: Simon & Schuster, 2000), 180.

[34] David Remnick and Henry Finder, editors, *Fierce Pajamas: Selections of Humor from an Anthology*

References

of Humor Writing from The New Yorker, (New York: Random House, 2001).

[35] Yo Yo Ma interviewed by Pam Belluck, "Your Brain on Music," *Science Times Podcast*, April 19, 2011, http://levitin.mcgill.ca/mediaplayer/radio.php.

[36] Robert McKee, *Story: Substance, Structure, Style and the Principles of Screenwriting*, (New York: HarperCollins 1997), Audible.com abridged edition.

[37] Sun Tzu, *The Art of War*, Edited by James Clavell (New York; Delacorte Press, 1983).

[38] *Id.*, Foreword by James Clavell, p. 3-5.

[39] Walt Disney's Disneyland, ABC, October 31, 1956, online videoclip. Last accessed March 7, 2012, http://www.youtube.com/watch?v=39z1MrlPYxE

[40] Ariston Anderson, "Francis Ford Copola on Risk, Money, Craft & Collaboration, *The 99%*, http://the99percent.com/articles/6973/Francis-Ford-Coppola-On-Risk-Money-Craft-Collaboration.

[41] Aileen Pincus, "The Perfect (Elevator) Pitch," *Bloomberg Business*, June 18, 2007, http://www.businessweek.com/careers/content/jun2007/ca20070618_134959.htm

[42] Doyle A. Rowland, United States Magistrate Judge, Sixth Judicial District, Kalamazoo, Michigan, (1939-2000).

[43] *Rashomon*, Dir. Akira Kurosawa, Daiei Motion Picture Company, 1950.

[44] John McPhee, *Annals of a Former World,* (New York: Farrar, Strauss, Giroux, 1981).

[45] John McPhee, "Progression, How and What?," *The New Yorker*, Nov 14, 2011, digital edition.

[46] John McPhee interview by Peter Hessler, "John McPhee, The Art of Non-Fiction No. 3," *Paris Review*, http://www.theparisreview.org/interviews/5997/the-art-of-nonfiction-no-3-john-mcphee, last accessed March 8, 2012.

[47] *Id.*

[48] John McPhee, *Oranges*, (New York: Farrar, Straus, Giroux, 1966).

[49] Chipp Reid, "Violence Halts Allsvanskan Derby," March 9, 2011, http://www.nordstjernan.com/news/sports/3378/

[50] Daniel H. Pink, *A Whole New Mind: Why Right Brainers Will Rule the Future* (New York: The Berkley Publishing Group, 2005), audible.com edition.

[51] Bill Bryson, *A Short History of Nearly Everything*, (London: Black Swan, 2003), 330.

[52] Daniel Kahneman, *Thinking, Fast and Slow*, (London, Eng: Penguin Books Ltd., 2011), 305.

[53] Muhtar Kent interviewed by Adi Ignatius, "Shaking Things Up at Coca Cola, " *HBR IdeaCast*, Sept 22, 2011, http://hbr.org/2011/10/shaking-things-up-at-coca-cola/ar/1?referral=00134

[54] *A Way with Words*, http://www.waywordradio.org/listen/

[55] Robert A. Harris, *Writing with Clarity and Style; A Guide to Rhetorical Devices*, (Los Angeles: Pyrczak Publishing, 2003), http://www.virtualsalt.com/rhetoric.htm

[56] Paraphrased from *The Spy Who Loved Me,* Dir. Lewis Gilbert, Based on the Novel by Ian Fleming, Eon Films, 1977.

[57] "Weakness of Character," *30 Rock*, NBC, Season 1, Episode 3, online video clip,

http://www.youtube.com/watch?v=Y_HvfIB8NEk

[58] Bill Waterson, *The Complete Calvin and Hobbes, Vol 3*, (Kansas City: Andrew McMeel Publishing, 2005), 31.

[59] Dr. Frank Luntz, *Words That Work: It's Not What You Say, It's What People Hear,* (New York: Hyperion, 2007).

[60] Gareth Morgan, *Images of Organization 2d Ed.* (Thousand Oaks: Sage Publication, 1997).

[61] Chris Gondek, *The Invisible Hand,* http://www.heronandcrane.com/TIH38051512.mp3

[62] "How to Slay a Cliché," December 22, 2011, http://cliche-a-day.blogspot.com/

[63] Dave Pilkey, *The Adventures of Captain Underpants*, (New York: The Blue Sky Press, 1997).

[64] "Many Eyes," http://www-958.ibm.com/software/data/cognos/manyeyes/

[65] Fred R. Shapiro, Ed., *Yale book of Quotations*, (Connecticut: Yale University Press, 2006).

[66] William Saffire, "Location, Location, Location," *New York Times Magazine*, June 26, 2009, http://www.nytimes.com/2009/06/28/magazine/28FOB
-onlanguage-t.html?_r=1&scp=1&sq=%22location%20location%0
22%20real%20estate%20chicago%2014&st=cse

[67] "Facts are stubborn things; and whatever may be our wishes, our inclinations, or the dictates of our passion, they cannot alter the state of facts and evidence."
http://www.brainyquote.com/quotes/authors/j/john_adams.html#ixzz1lGTDdlFq

[68] Eleanor Roosevelt, http://www.quotationspage.com/quote/35592.html

[69] "101 Football Quotes," *Football Babble*, http://www.footballbabble.com/football/college/quotes/

[70] Matthew Rabin and Joel L. Schrag, "First Impressions Matter: A Model of Confirmatory Bias," *The Quarterly Journal of Economics*, February 1999, 37-82; Elazar J. Pedhazur, Liora Pedhazur Schmelkin, *Measurement, Design, and Analysis: An Integrated Approach*, (Hillsdale, New Jersey: Lawrence Erlbaum Associates, Inc., 1991).

[71] Harold Bloom, *Stories and Poems for Extremely Intelligent Children of All Ages*, (New York: Touchstone, 2001), 60.

[72] Kurt Vonnegut, The Shapes of Stories,
http://www.youtube.com/watch?v=oP3c1h8v2ZQ&feature=player_embedded; *see also* "Kurt Vonnegut at the Blackboard," *Lapham's Quarterly*, New York City, 2005

[73] *Dragnet*, creator and producer, Jack Webb, NBC, 1967.

[74] Foreword by Tom Wolfe, *The New Journalism*, (London: Picador, 1975), 35.

[75] Pantone LLC, http://www.pantone.com/pages/pantone/category.aspx?ca=88

[76] "A general limitation of the human mind is it imperfect ability to reconstruct past states of knowledge, or beliefs that have changed." Daniel Kahneman, *Thinking Fast and Slow*, (New York: Farrar, Strauss & Giroux), p 202.

[77] Sir Arthur Conan Doyle, "A Case of Identity," *The Adventures of Sherlock Holmes*, iBook version, p. 129.

References

[78] David Wagner, "Speaking in Tongues," *MIT Sloan Management Review, The Magazine*, July 1, 2006, online version, http://sloanreview.mit.edu/the-magazine/2006-summer/47401/speaking-in-tongues-2/

[79] Elmore Leonard, *10 Rules of Writing*, (New York: HarperCollins, 2001).

[80] John McPhee interview by Peter Hessler, *Paris Review*, note 44.

[81] Meagan O'Rouke, "The Sweetest Sounds I Ever Read," *Wall Street Journal*, online version, February 26, 2011, http://online.wsj.com/article/SB10001424052748703529004576160322387772618.html

[82] Michael Frishkopf and Kristina Nelson interviewed by Banning Eyre, "Koranic Recitation," 2011, *Afropop Worldwide*, http://www.afropop.org/multi/interview/ID/212

[83] Kahneman, *Thinking Fast and Slow*, p. 63.

[84] http://grammar.quickanddirtytips.com/

[85] R.L.G., "The dreaded comma splice," "Language," *The Economist*, online version, January 10, 2012, http://www.economist.com/blogs/johnson/2012/01/punctuation?fsrc=nlw|newe|1-11-2012|new_on_the_economist#sort-comments

[86] Sebastian Junger, *The Perfect Storm* (W.W. Norton & Co., 1997).

[87] John Vorhaus, *The Comic Toolbox* (Los Angeles: Silman-James Press, 1994).

www.ingramcontent.com/pod-product-compliance
Lightning Source LLC
Chambersburg PA
CBHW051512170526
45166CB00001B/489